From Knit to
Crochet™

How to get the look and feel of knitting with crochet!

The Needlecraft® Shop

Contents

Introduction

If you have ever drooled over the designs in knitting books and magazines, and wished you could find the same stylish looks in crochet—this book is for you! Each of our crochet projects started with a favorite knit pattern stitch. Then the designer developed that same look using her crochet hook.

If you would like to take these crochet pattern stitches and develop projects of your own, we've given the pattern stitch for you to use. But if you would rather leave the designing to others, the stars of this book are the outstanding garments and home decor creations. You'll be amazed at the wide variety of stitch patterns and how closely they resemble their knitted origins.

From Knit to Crochet © 2005 The Needlecraft Shop, Berne, Indiana 46711 All rights reserved. No part of this publication may be reproduced or transmitted in any form or by any means, electronic or mechanical, including photocopying, recording, or any other information storage and retrieval system, without the written permission of the publisher.

Editor: Bobbie Matela
Art Director: Brad Snow
Publishing Services Manager:
   Brenda Gallmeyer
Associate Editors: Kathy Wesley,
   Mary Ann Frits
Copy Supervisor: Michelle Beck
Copy Editors: Conor Allen, Mary Martin
Technical Artist: Chad Summers

Book & Cover Design: Karen Allen
Graphic Artist Supervisor: Ronda Bechinski
Graphic Artist: Vicki Staggs
Production Assistants: Cheryl Kempf,
   Marj Morgan

Photography Supervisor: Tammy Christian
Photography: Carl Clark, Christena Green,
   Matt Owen
Photography Stylist: Tammy Nussbaum

Chief Executive Officer: John Robinson
Publishing Director: David McKee
Book Marketing Director: Craig Scott
Editorial Director: Vivian Rothe
Publishing Services Director:
   Brenda R. Wendling

Printed in China
First Printing: 2005
Library of Congress Number: 2004111906
Hardcover ISBN: 1-57367-177-0
Softcover ISBN: 1-57367-190-8

Every effort has been made to ensure the accuracy and completeness of the instructions in this book. However, we cannot be responsible for human error or for the results when using materials other than those specified in the instructions, or for variations in individual work.
1 2 3 4 5 6 7 8 9

Chapter 1
Before You Begin

Here's some background information that will get you off to a successful start. Whether creating your own original design or recreating one of the designs in this book, here's what you need to know.

Before You Begin

Yarns & Gauges

We've taken knit patterns—from eleborate to simple—and converted them into crochet patterns. The stitch pattern for each crochet version is given along with a project using that stitch pattern.

To achieve the same look as our project, we have indicated the yarn we used. Other yarns of the same weight can be substituted, but first make a swatch with that yarn to be sure it has the desired look. The yarn, hook size and gauge are very important to the finished product. The extra time taken before beginninng is well worth it to have a finished project that will be what you envisioned.

For a gauge swatch, check the pattern for the recommended-size hook. Chain enough stitches to work up a sample swatch that will be at least 4 inches long. This allows for enough stitches to most accurately measure the gauge.

Work the swatch in the stitch listed in the pattern under "Gauge" until you have a 4-inch square. Fasten off the yarn.

Place the swatch on a flat surface and measure the piece in the center area to avoid the distortion of the edges. You should have the number of stitches and rows indicated under "Gauge."

Since each of us crochets differently, your gauge may not match the one listed. In that case, you need to make adjustments in hook size until the same gauge is achieved. If the number of stitches and rows are fewer than indicated, your hook is too large. Try another swatch with a smaller-size hook. If the number of stitches and rows are more than indicated, your hook is too small. Try another swatch with a larger-size hook.

If you want to use the stitch pattern to develop your own original design, the first step is to make a gauge swatch using your yarn choice. Once you like the look of your swatch, you can use the gauge to plan your project.

Drawing & Working With Schematics

A schematic is a small-scale diagram of finished garment pieces before assembly. They are normally used for clothing patterns, but can also be used for afghans, and other items that must be sized to fit together properly.

The schematics with our patterns can offer valuable information at a glance about measurements of completed pieces, as well as shape and correct positioning of pieces for blocking and assembly.

When using a crochet stitch pattern to design a garment with shaped areas, it is helpful to draw a schematic for yourself. Draw a rough outline of the shape of each piece of the finished item—graph paper is often helpful. Calculate the number of stitches or rows needed in the various sections by multiplying the stitch or row gauge by the measurements of the section and mark each on the drawing. Then as you crochet the piece, compare the schematic to your work to be sure your piece is developing the proper shaping.

Use a clothing schematic to your advantage by comparing body measurements of the person who will wear the garment to the diagram. Measuring garments already owned can be a valuable aid in deciding the dimensions of your new design.

These garment measurements are important to finished style and fit:

1. Chest/bust: width across front or back at chest or bust (add front and back together for total).

2. Bottom ribbing: width of ribbing.

3. Shoulder: width of shoulder from neck edge to armhole edge.

4. Armhole: depth from shoulder straight down to bottom of the armhole.

5. Across back: width across the upper back at shoulders.

6. Side body: length from bottom edge to underarm.

7. Back length: length from bottom edge to base of neck at center back.

8. Underarm sleeve: length of sleeve from underarm to bottom edge.

9. Upper arm: circumference around sleeve at upper arm.

10. Sleeve ribbing: width of sleeve ribbing.

Creating an Original

Having checked the gauge in yarn you like and having drawn a schematic, you can now work with the multiples in the stitch pattern to create your own original. The first number in the multiple given for the stitch pattern tells you the number of stitches in each repeat of the pattern. The second number is the number of additional chains needed for the beginning chain.

If creating your own pattern is a new challenge for you, the best place to begin is with an afghan. Decide how wide you want the afghan to be and make a swatch using the pattern stitch as given. Measure the width of the swatch for one repeat of the pattern. Divide the finished width you want for your afghan by the width of the repeat. The resulting number tells you how many times you need to repeat the pattern stitch to achieve the desired width for your afghan. You may have to round the number up or down to get a whole number. Then multiply the number of repeats by the number of stitches in the pattern repeat and add the additional number to get the number of stitches needed for the beginning chain.

After working the beginning chain begin with Row 1 of the pattern, repeating it across the number of times you calculated. Continue working the pattern until the afghan is the desired length. Once you start using these patterns, there are all sorts of new opportunities. A pattern repeat can be centered on a sweater front or sleeve, or pattern stitches can be combined for a totally different look.

As long as a gauge swatch is made first, the yarn and hook size can be changed to get a new look for your creation.

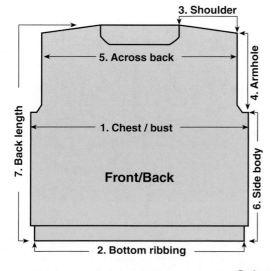
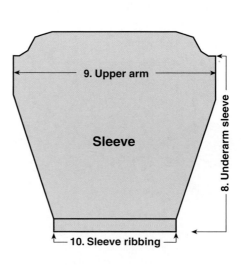

Schematics

Seams & Joinings

Quality finishing is an important step in producing beautiful hand-crafted items. Even a well-stitched item will be less attractive if the seams are bulky or uneven.

Different seams should be used depending on the type of yarn and stitches used. Also consider the location of the seam if making a garment.

Experiment with several methods for each seam. After becoming familiar with the various seams, you'll be able to choose seams that make your crocheted items stand out among the very best.

The pattern usually lists the order in which to assemble the pieces. A few pins before sewing helps in the matching of stitches and rows. Use yarn the same color as the pieces being sewn, and if possible, change yarn colors when the stitch color changes. In some cases the yarn may be too thick for sewing, in which case use a thinner yarn in a matching color.

A good seam for joining pieces edge-to-edge is the **woven seam**. It gives a smooth and neat appearance, as it weaves the edges together from the right side.

Thread a tapestry needle with matching yarn and attach the yarn to both pieces at the beginning of the seam. Weave the needle back and forth joining the two pieces as shown in Photo A. At the end of the seam secure and hide the yarn.

A woven seam can also be used to sew the tops of stitches and/or starting chains together. Just insert the needle through the tops of the stitches of through the chain rather than through the ends of the rows.

On some types of items, an **overcast seam** may be used. This method is often well-suited for cotton or thinner yarns. As on the woven seam the stiches or rows are aligned before starting, however, the overcast seam is worked on the wrong side. The needle is always inserted in the same direction through matching stitches (Photo B). This brings the yarn back over the seam each time a new stitch is made and provides a sturdier seam.

B

A **backstitch seam** is commonly used for joining pieces where there is a seam allowance. This is helpful when a slightly larger piece is to be eased to fit a smaller piece. However, this type of seam also adds more bulk to the seam. This seam is work on the wrong side with right sides held together. For each stitch, insert the needle as shown, then bring the needle back through. (Photo C). ❖

A

C

Chapter 2
Afghans

Not only will these afghans add warmth and coziness to your home, they are also a great way to add texture and color to your decorating scheme.

Twisted & Crossed Cables

A special, front post stitch is the secret to creating this beautiful pattern.

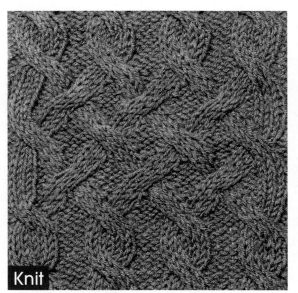
Knit

Crochet

Crochet Stitch Pattern

Special Stitches

For **front post half double crochet (fphdc),** yo, insert hook from front to back around post (see Stitch Guide) of st indicated, yo, draw lp through, yo, draw through 3 lps on hook.

For **front cable,** sk next 3 sts, fpdc around each of next 3 post sts *(mark last st made to avoid missing 1 of the 2 center sts when working back across the row);* working in front of last 3 post sts made, fpdc around each of 3 skipped sts.

For **back cable,** sk next 3 sts, fpdc around each of next 3 post sts *(mark last st made to avoid missing 1 of the 2 center sts when working back across the row);* working behind last

3 post sts made, fpdc around each of 3 skipped sts.

Multiple of 70 sts + 1

Row 1: Loosely ch 71, sc in 2nd ch from hook, sc in next ch, [(sc, hdc) in next ch, hdc in next 4 chs, (hdc, sc) in next ch, sc in next 2 chs] 4 times, sc in next 4 chs, [(sc, hdc) in next ch, hdc in next 4 chs, (hdc, sc) in next ch, sc in next 2 chs] 4 times, turn. *(70 sts)*

Row 2 (RS): Ch 1, sc in first 3 sts, [**fphdc** *(see Special Stitches)* around each of next 6 hdc, sc in next 4 sts] 4 times, sc in next 4 sts, [fphdc around each of next 6 hdc,

sc in next 4 sts] 3 times; fphdc around each of next 6 hdc, sc in last 3 sts, turn.

Row 3 & all odd-numbered rows: Ch 1, sc in each st across, turn.

Row 4: Ch 1, sc in first 3 sts, [fphdc around next 6 post sts on row before last, sc in next 4 sc] 4 times, sc in next 4 sc, [fphdc around next 6 post sts on row before last, sc in next 4 sc] 3 times, fphdc around next 6 post sts, sc in last 3 sc, turn.

Row 6: Ch 1, sc in first 3 sc, [**front cable** *(see Special Stitches),* sk next 6 sc, sc in next 4 sc] 4 times, sc in next 4 sc, [front cable, sk next 6 sc, sc in next 4 sc] 3 times, front cable, sk next 6 sc, sc in last 3 sc, turn.

Rows 8 & 10: Rep Row 4.

Row 12: Rep Row 6.

Row 14: Ch 1, sc in first 3 sts, fphdc around next 3 post sts, sk next 3 sts, sc in next st, fphdc around next 3 post sts, sk next 3 sts, [sc in next 2 sts, fphdc around next 3 post sts, sk next 3 sts, sc in next 2 sts, fphdc around next 3 post sts, sk next 3 sts] 2 times, sc in next 2 sts, fphdc around next 3 post sts, sk next 3 sts, sc in next st, fphdc around next 3 post sts, sk next 3 sts, sc in next 8 sts, fphdc around next 3 post sts, sk next 3 sts, sc in next st, fphdc around next 3 post sts, sk next 3 sts, [sc in next 2 sts, fphdc around next 3 post sts, sk next 3 sts, sc in next 2 sts, fphdc around next 3 post sts, sk next 3 sts] 2 times, sc in next 2 sts, fphdc around next 3 post sts, sk next 3 sts, sc in next st, fphdc around next 3 post sts, sk next 3 sts, sc in last 3 sts, turn.

Row 16: Ch 1, sc in first 3 sts, fphdc around next 3 post sts, sk next 3 sc, sc in next 2 sts, [fphdc around next 6 post sts, sk next 6 sts, sc in next 4 sts] 2 times, fphdc around next 6 post sts, sk next 6 sts, sc in next 2 sts, fphdc around next 3 post sts, sc in next 8 sts,

fphdc around next 3 post sts, sk next 3 sts, sc in next 2 sts, [fphdc around next 6 post sts, sk next 6 sts, sc in next 4 sts] 2 times, fphdc around next 6 post sts, sk next 6 sts, sc in next 2 sts, fphdc around next 3 post sts, sc in last 3 sc, turn.

Row 18: Ch 1, sc in first 3 sts, fphdc around next 3 post sts, sk next 3 sts, sc in next 2 sts, [back cable *(see Special Stitches),* sk next 6 sts, sc in next 4 sts] 2 times, back cable, sk next 6 sts, sc in next 2 sts, fphdc around next 3 post sts, sk next 3 sts, sc in next 8 sts, [**back cable**, sk next 6 sts, sc in next 4 sts] 2 times, back cable, sk next 6 sts, sc in next 2 sts, fphdc around next 3 post sts, sk next 3 sts, sc in last 3 sc, turn.

Row 20: Ch 1, sc in first 3 sts, fphdc around next 3 post sts, sk next 3 sts, sc in next st, fphdc around next 3 post sts, sk next 3 sts, [sc in next 2 sts, fphdc around next 3 post sts, sk next 3 sts] 5 times, sc in next st, fphdc around next 3 post sts, sk next 3 sts, sc in next 8 sts, fphdc around next 3 post sts, sk next 3 sts, sc in next st, fphdc around next 3 post sts, sk next 3 sts, [sc in next 2 sts, fphdc around next 3 post sts, sk next 3 sts] 5 times, sc in next st, fphdc around next 3 post sts, sk next 3 sts, sc in last 3 sts, turn.

Row 22: Ch 1, sc in first 3 sts, fphdc around next 6 post sts, sk next 6 sts, [sc in next 4 sts, fphdc around next 6 post sts, sk next 6 sts] 3 times, sc in next 8 sts, fphdc around next 6 post sts, sk next 6 sts, [sc in next 4 sts, fphdc around next 6 post sts, sk next 6 sts] 3 times, sc in last 3 sts, turn.

Row 24: Ch 1, sc in first 3 sts, front cable, sk next 6 sts, [sc in next 4 sts, front cable, sk next 6 sts] 3 times, sc in next 8 sts; front cable, sk next 6 sts, [sc in next 4 sts, front cable, sk next 6 sts] 3 times, sc in last 3 sts, turn.

Rows 26–37: Rep Rows 14–25.

Rows 38 & 40: Ch 1, sc in first 3 sts, fphdc around next 6 post sts, sk next 6 sts, [sc in next 4 sts, fphdc around next 6 post sts, sk next 6 sts] 3 times, sc in next 8 sc, fphdc around next 6 post sts, sk next 6 sts, [sc in next 4 sts, fphdc around next 6 post sts, sk next 6 sts] 3 times, sc in last 3 sts, turn.

Row 42: Ch 1, sc in first 3 sts, front cable, sk next 6 sc, [sc in next 4 sts, front cable, sk next 6 sts] 3 times, sc in next 8 sts, front cable, sk next 6 sc, [sc in next 4 sts, front cable, sk next 6 sts] 3 times, sc in last 3 sts, turn.

Row 44: Ch 1, sc in first 3 sts, fphdc around next 6 post sts, sk next 6 sts, [sc in next 4 sts, fphdc around next 6 post sts, sk next 6 sts] 3

times, sc in next 8 sts, fphdc around next 6 post sts, sk next 6 sts, [sc in next 4 sts, fphdc around next 6 post sts, sk next 6 sts] 3 times, sc in last 3 sts, turn.

Rows 45–54: [Rep Rows 3 and 4] 5 times.

Rep Rows 3–54 for pattern.

Note: For sc dec, pull up lp in next 2 sts, yo, draw through all 3 lps on hook.

Last row: Ch 1, sc in first st, [**sc dec** (*see Note*) over next 2 sts, fphdc in next 6 sts, sc dec over next 2 sts] 4 times, sc in next 4 sts, [sc dec over next 2 sts, fphdc in next 6 sts, sc dec over next 2 sts] 4 times, sc in last st. Fasten off.

Twisted & Crossed Cables Afghan

Design by Donna Jones

This spectacular afghan can be created in any color that fits your decorating scheme. It is shown here in light denim blue for a casual look, but could have a more elegant look in a neutral tone.

 INTERMEDIATE

Finished Size
Approximately 44 x 60 inches

Materials
Coats & Clark Red Heart TLC Heathers medium (worsted) weight yarn:
50 oz/2770 yds/1500g
#2474 light denim
Bobby pins for markers
Size I/9/5.5mm crochet hook or size needed to obtain gauge

Gauge
6 sc = 2 inches; 6 sc rows = 2 inches

Row 1: Loosely ch 107, sc in 2nd ch from hook, sc in next ch, *[(sc, hdc) in next ch,

hdc in next 4 chs, (hdc, sc) in next ch, sc in next 2 chs] 4 times, sc in next 4 chs; rep from * once more; [(sc, hdc) in next ch, hdc in next 4 chs, (hdc, sc) in next ch, sc in next 2 chs] 4 times, turn. *(130 sts)*

Row 2: Ch 1, sc in first 3 sts, *[**fphdc** (*see Special Stitches on page 10*) around each of next 6 hdc, sc in next 4 sts] 4 times, sc in next 4 sts; rep from * once more; [fphdc around each of next 6 hdc, sc in next 4 sts] 3 times, fphdc around each of next 6 hdc, sc in last 3 sts, turn.

Row 3 & all odd-numbered rows: Ch 1, sc in each st across, turn.

Row 4: Ch 1, sc in first 3 sts, *[fphdc around next 6 post sts on row before last, sc in next 4 sts] 4 times, sc in next 4 sts; rep from * once more; [fphdc around next 6 post sts on row before last, sc in next 4 sts] 3 times, fphdc around next 6 post sts, sc in last 3 sts, turn.

Row 6: Ch 1, sc in first 3 sts, *[**front cable** *(see Special Stitches on page 10),* sk next 6 sts, sc in next 4 sts] 4 times, sc in next 4 sts; rep from * once more; [front cable, sk next 6 sts, sc in next 4 sts] 3 times, front cable, sk next 6 sts, sc in last 3 sts, turn.

Rows 8 & 10: Rep Row 4.

Row 12: Rep Row 6.

Row 14: Ch 1, sc in first 3 sts, *fphdc around next 3 post sts, sk next 3 sts, sc in next st, fphdc around next 3 post sts, sk next 3 sts, [sc in next 2 sts, fphdc around next 3 post sts, sk next 3 sts, sc in next 2 sts, fphdc around next 3 post sts, sk next 3 sts] 2 times, sc in next 2 sts, fphdc around next 3 post sts, sk next 3 sts, sc in next st, fphdc around next 3 post sts, sk next 3 sts, sc in next 8 sts; rep from * once more; fphdc around next 3 post sts, sk next 3 sts, sc in next st, fphdc around next 3 post sts, sk next 3 sts, [sc in next 2 sts, fphdc around next 3 post sts, sk next 3 sts, sc in next 2 sts, fphdc around next 3 post sts, sk next 3 sts] 2 times, sc in next 2 sts, fphdc around next 3 post sts, sk next 3 sts, sc in next st, fphdc around next 3 post sts, sk next 3 sts, sc in last 3 sts, turn.

Row 16: Ch 1, sc in first 3 sts, *fphdc around next 3 post sts, sk next 3 sts, sc in next 2 sts, [fphdc around next 6 post sts, sk next 6 sts, sc in next 4 sts] 2 times, fphdc around next 6 post sts, sk next 6 sts, sc in next 2 sts, fphdc around next 3 post sts, sc in next 8 sts; rep from * once more; fphdc around next 3 post sts, sk next 3 sts, sc in next 2 sts, [fphdc around next 6 post sts, sk next 6 sts, sc in next 4 sts] 2 times, fphdc around next 6 post sts, sk next 6 sts, sc in next 2 sts, fphdc around next 3 post sts, sc in last 3 sts, turn.

Row 18: Ch 1, sc in first 3 sts, fphdc around next 3 post sts, sk next 3 sts, sc in next 2 sts, next *[back 6 sts, **back cable** *(see Special Stitches on page 10),* sk next 6 sts, sc in next 4 sts] 2 times, back cable, sk next 6 sts, sc in next 2 sts, fphdc around next 3 post sts, sk next 3 sts, sc in next 8 sts; rep from * once more; [back cable, sk next 6 sts, sc in next 4 sts] 2 times, back cable, sk next 6 sts, sc in next 2 sts, fphdc around next 3 post sts, sk next 3 sts, sc in last 3 sts, turn.

Row 20: Ch 1, sc in first 3 sts, *fphdc around next 3 post sts, sk next 3 sts, sc in next st, fphdc around next 3 post sts, sk next 3 sts, [sc in next 2 sts, fphdc around next 3 post sts, sk next 3 sts] 5 times, sc in next st, fphdc around next 3 post sts, sk next 3 sts, sc in next 8 sts; rep from * once more; fphdc around next 3 post sts, sk next 3 sts, sc in next st, fphdc around next 3 post sts, sk next 3 sts, [sc in next 2 sts, fphdc around next 3 post sts, sk next 3 sts] 5 times, sc in next st, fphdc around next 3 post sts, sk next 3 sts, sc in last 3 sts, turn.

Row 22: Ch 1, sc in first 3 sts, *fphdc around next 6 post sts, sk next 6 sts, [sc in next 4 sts, fphdc around next 6 post sts, sk next 6 sts] 3 times, sc in next 8 sts; rep from * once more; fphdc around next 6 post sts, sk next 6 sts, [sc in next 4 sts, fphdc around next 6 post sts, sk next 6 sts] 3 times, sc in last 3 sts, turn.

Row 24: Ch 1, sc in first 3 sts, *front cable, sk next 6 sts, [sc in next 4 sts, front cable, sk next 6 sts] 3 times, sc in next 8 sts; rep from * once more; front cable, sk next 6 sts, [sc in next 4 sts, front cable, sk next 6 sts] 3 times, sc in last 3 sts, turn.

Rows 26–37: Rep Rows 14–25.

Rows 38 & 40: Ch 1, sc in first 3 sts, *fphdc around next 6 post sts, sk next 6 sts, [sc in next 4 sts, fphdc around next 6 post sts, sk next 6 sts] 3 times, sc in next 8 sts; rep from * once more, fphdc around next 6 post sts, sk next 6 sts, [sc in next 4 sts, fphdc around next 6 post sts, sk next 6 sts] 3 times, sc in last 3 sts, turn.

Row 42: Ch 1, sc in first 3 sts, *front cable, sk next 6 sts, [sc in next 4 sts, front cable, sk next 6 sts] 3 times, sc in next 8 sts; rep from * once more; front cable, sk next 6 sts, [sc in next 4 sts, front cable, sk next 6 sts] 3 times, sc in last 3 sts, turn.

Row 44: Ch 1, sc in first 3 sts, *fphdc around next 6 post sts, sk next 6 sts, [sc in next 4 sts, fphdc around next 6 post sts, sk next 6 sts] 3 times, sc in next 8 sts; rep from * once more; fphdc around next 6 post sts, sk next 6 sts, [sc in next 4 sts, fphdc around next 6 post sts, sk next 6 sts] 3 times, sc in last 3 sts, turn.

Rows 45–54: [Rep Rows 3 and 4] 5 times.

Rep Rows 3–54 until afghan measures approximately 60 inches, or desired length, ending with Row 44.

Note: For sc dec, pull up lp in next 2 sts, yo, draw through all 3 lps on hook.

Last row: Ch 1, sc in first st, *[**sc dec** (*see Note*) over next 2 sts, fphdc in next 6 sts, sc dec over next 2 sts] 4 times, sc in next 4 sts; rep from * once more; [sc dec over next 2 sts, fphdc in next 6 sts, sc dec over next 2 sts] 4 times, sc in last sc. Fasten off.

Fringe

For each **knot,** cut 2 strands 12 inches long. Holding both strands tog as 1, fold in half, insert hook from back to front through st, pull fold through st, pull ends through fold, pull snug.

Knot fringe in each corner and in every 3rd st across first and last rows. Trim ends even. ❖

Steep Chevron

Front post half double crochet stitches combine with single crochets to form the deep peaks and valleys of this subtly textured pattern.

Knit

Crochet

Crochet Stitch Pattern

Special Stitch

For **front post half double crochet (fphdc),** yo, insert hook from front to back around post *(see Stitch Guide)* of st indicated, yo, draw lp through, yo, draw through all lps on hook.

Multiple of 18 sts + 2

Row 1: Ch 20, sc in 2nd ch from hook and in each ch across, turn. *(19 sc)*

Row 2 & all even-numbered rows: Ch 1, sc in each sc across, turn.

Rows 3 & 5: Ch 1, sc in first st, [**fphdc** *(see Special Stitch)* around each of next 2 sts on row before last, sk next 2 sts on last row, sc in next 2 sts] 2 times, fphdc around next st on row before last, sk next st on last row, [sc in next 2 sts, fphdc around each of next 2 sts on row before last, sk next 2 sts on last row] 2 times, sc in last st, turn.

Rows 7 & 9: Ch 1, sc in first 2 sts, fphdc around each of next 2 sts on row before last, sk next 2 sts on last row, sc in next 2 sts, fphdc around each of next 2 sts on row before last, sk next 2 sts on last row, sc in next 3 sts, fphdc around each of next 2 sts on row before last, sk next 2 sts on last row, sc in next 2 sts, fphdc around each of next 2 sts on row before last, sk next 2 sts on last row, sc in last 2 sts, turn.

Rows 11 & 13: Ch 1, sc in first 3 sts, fphdc

around each of next 2 sts on row before last, sk next 2 sts on last row, sc in next 2 sts, fphdc around each of next 2 sts on row before last, sk next 2 sts on last row, sc in next st, fphdc around next 2 sts on row before last, sk next 2 sts on last row, sc in next 2 sts, fphdc around next 2 sts on row before last, sk next 2 sts on last row, sc in last 3 sts, turn.

Rows 15 & 17: Ch 1, sc in first st, fphdc around next st on row before last, sk next st on last row, sc in next 2 sts, fphdc around each of next 2 sts on row before last, sk next 2 sts on last row, sc in next 2 sts, fphdc around each of next 3 sts on row before last, sk next 3 sts on last row, sc in next 2 sts, fphdc around each of next 2 sts on row

before last, sk next 2 sts on last row, sc in next 2 sts, fphdc around next st on row before last, sk next st on last row, sc in last st, turn.

Rows 19 & 21: Ch 1, sc in first st, [fphdc around each of next 2 sts on row before last, sk next 2 sts on row below, sc in next 2 sts] 2 times, fphdc around next st on row before last, sk next st on last row, [sc in next 2 sts, fphdc around each of next 2 sts on row before last, sk next 2 sts on last row] 2 times, sc in last st, turn.

Row 22: Ch 1, sc in each st across, turn.

Rep Rows 7–22 for pattern, ending with Row 13.

Steep Chevron Afghan

Design by Darla Sims

Classically crocheted in fisherman yarn, this afghan will be at home in a wide variety of home decor styles. It is a wonderful choice for gift giving.

 **INTERMEDIATE**

Finished Size
Approximately 48 x 62 inches

Materials
Lion Brand Wool-Ease medium (worsted) weight yarn:

[**4** MEDIUM]

51 oz/3349 yds/1445g #99 fisherman
Size H/8/5mm and I/9/5.5mm crochet hooks or sizes needed to obtain gauge

Gauge
With larger hook:
1 pattern rep = 6 inches

Row 1: With larger hook, loosely ch 146, sc in 2nd ch from hook and in each ch across, turn. *(145 sc)*

Row 2 & all even-numbered rows: Ch 1, sc in each sc across, turn.

Rows 3 & 5: Ch 1, sc in first st, *[**fphdc** *(see Special Stitch on page 16)* around each of next 2 sts on row before last, sk next 2 sts on last row, sc in next 2 sts] 2 times, fphdc around next st on row before last, sk next st on last row, [sc in next 2 sts, fphdc around each of next 2 sts on row before last, sk next 2 sts on last row] 2 times, sc in next st; rep from * 7 times more, turn.

Rows 7 & 9: Ch 1, sc in first 2 sts, *fphdc around each of next 2 sts on row before last, sk next 2 sts on last row, sc in next 2 sts, fphdc around each of next 2 sts on row before last, sk next 2 sts on last row, sc in next 3 sts; rep from * 14 times more, fphdc around each of next 2 sts on row before last, sk next 2 sts on last row, sc in next 2 sts, fphdc around each of next 2 sts on row before last, sk next 2 sts on last row, sc in last 2 sts, turn.

Rows 11 & 13: Ch 1, sc in first 3 sts, *fphdc around each of next 2 sts on row before last, sk next 2 sts on last row, sc in next 2 sts, fphdc around each of next 2 sts on row before last, sk next 2 sts on last row, sc in next st, [fphdc around next 2 sts on row before last, sk next 2 sts on last row, sc in next 2 sts] 2 times, fphdc around next st on row before last, sk next st on last row, sc in next 2 sts; rep from * 6 times more, fphdc around each of next 2 sts on row before last, sk next 2 sts on last row, sc in next 2 sts, fphdc around each of next 2 sts on row before last, sk next 2 sts on last row, sc in next st, [fphdc around next 2 sts on row before last, sk next 2 sts on last row, sc in next 2 sts] 2 times, sc in last st, turn.

Rows 15 & 17: Ch 1, sc in first st, fphdc around next st, sk next st on last row, *sc in next 2 sts, fphdc around each of next 2 sts on row before last, sk next 2 sts on last row, sc in next 2 sts, fphdc around each of next 3 sts on row before last, sk next 3 sts on last row; rep from * 14 times more, sc in next 2 sts, fphdc around each of next 2 sts on row before last, sk next 2 sts on last row, sc in next 2 sts,

fphdc around next st on row before last, sk next st on last row, sc in last st, turn.

Rows 19 & 21: Ch 1, sc in first st, *[fphdc around each of next 2 sts on row before last, sk next 2 sts on row below, sc in next 2 sts] 2 times, fphdc around next st on row before last, sk next st on last row, [sc in next 2 sts, fphdc around each of next 2 sts on row before last, sk next 2 sts on last row] 2 times, sc in next st, rep from * 7 times more, turn.

Row 22: Ch 1, sc in each st across, turn.

Rep Rows 3–22 until afghan measures 58 inches or desired length, ending with Row 13. Fasten off.

Edging
Rnd 1: With smaller hook and RS of work facing, join yarn in first st in upper right-hand corner, ch 1, 3 sc in same st, sc in each st and in end of each row around afghan and work 3 sc in each corner; join with sl st in first st.

Rnd 2: *Ch 30, sc in next st; rep from * around; join with sl st in first ch. Fasten off. ♣

Entwined Cables

This interesting pattern of cables is created with single crochet stitches and front post double and triple crochet stitches.

Knit

Crochet

Crochet Stitch Pattern

Special Stitches

For **front post double crochet (fpdc),** yo, insert hook from front to back around post *(see Stitch Guide)* of st indicated, yo, draw lp through, (yo, draw through 2 lps on hook) 2 times.

For **front post treble crochet (fptr),** yo twice, insert hook from front to back around post *(see Stitch Guide)* of st indicated, yo, draw lp through, (yo, draw through 2 lps on hook) 3 times.

For **cable,** sk next 2 post sts on row before last, fptr *(see above)* around next 2 post sts, fptr around each skipped post st.

Multiple of 16 + 1

Row 1: With larger hook and A, loosely ch 17, sc in 2nd ch from hook and in each rem ch, turn. *(16 sc)*

Row 2 & all even-numbered rows: Ch 1, sc in each st across, turn.

Row 3: Ch 1, sc in first 2 sts, sk first 4 sts on row before last, **fpdc** *(see Special Stitches)* around each of next 2 sts on row before last, fpdc around each skipped st, sk next 4 sts on last row, sc in next 4 sts, sk next 6 sts on row before last from last fpdc, fpdc around each of next 2 sts, fpdc around each skipped st, sk next 4 sts on last row, sc in last 2 sts, turn.

Row 5: Ch 1, sc in first 2 sts, fpdc around next 2 post sts on row before last, sk next 2 sts on last row, sc in next 2 sts, fpdc around

next 4 post sts on row before last, sk next 4 sts on last row, sc in next 2 sc, fpdc around next 2 post sts on row before last, sk next 2 sts on last row, sc in last 2 sts, turn.

Row 7: Ch 1, sc in first 2 sts, fpdc around next 2 post sts on row before last, sk next 2 sts on last row, sc in next 2 sts, **cable** *(see Special Stitches),* sk next 4 sts on last row, sc in next 2 sts, fpdc around next 2 post sts on row before last, sc in last 2 sts, turn.

Row 9: Ch 1, sc in first 2 sts, fpdc around next 2 post sts on row before last, sk next 2 sts on last row, sc in next 2 sts, fpdc around next 4 post sts on row before last, sk next 4 sts on last row, sc in next 2 sts, fpdc around next 2 post sts on row before last, sk next 2 sts on last row, sc in last 2 sts, turn.

Row 11: Ch 1, sc in first 2 sts, fpdc around next 2 post sts on row before last, sk next 2 sts on last row, sc in next 2 sts, cable, sk next 4 sts on last row, sc in next 2 sts, fpdc around

next 2 post sts on row before last, sk next 2 sts on last row, sc in last 2 sts, turn.

Row 12: Ch 1, sc in each st across, turn.

Rows 13–20: [Rep Rows 11 and 12] 4 times.

Row 21: Ch 1, sc in first 2 sts, cable, sk next 4 sts on last row, sc in next 4 sts, cable, sc in last 2 sts, turn.

Row 23: Ch 1, sc in first 2 sts, fpdc around next 4 post sts on row before last, sk next 4 sts on last row, sc in next 4 sts, fpdc around next 4 post sts on row before last, sk next 4 sts on last row, sc in last 2 sts, turn.

Row 25: Ch 1, sc in first 2 sts, cable, sk next 4 sts on last row, sc in next 4 sts, cable, sk next 4 sts on last row, sc in last 2 sts, turn.

Row 26: Ch 1, sc in each st across, turn.

Rep Rows 5–26 for pattern.

Entwined Cables Afghan

Design by Darla Sims

Made in a bright shade of bulky weight yarn, this show-stopping design works up quickly and is fun to have around for cuddly warmth.

 INTERMEDIATE

Finished Size
38 x 49 inches

Materials
Lion Brand Kool Wool bulky (chunky) weight yarn:
    60 oz/2040 yds/1800g
      #186 melon (A)
    3½ oz/120 yds/105g
      #098 ivory (B)
Sizes J/10/6mm and K/10½/6.5mm crochet hooks or sizes needed to obtain gauge

Gauge
5 sts = 2 inches

Special Stitch
For **cluster (cl),** (yo, insert hook from front to back around post of next st and draw lp through) 3 times, yo and draw through all 4 lps on hook.

Row 1: With larger hook and A, loosely ch 97, sc in 2nd ch from hook and in each rem ch, turn. *(96 sc)*

Row 2 & all even-numbered rows: Ch 1, sc in each st, turn.

Row 3: Ch 1, sc in first 2 sts, sk next 2 sts on row before last, *__fpdc__ *(see Special Stitches on page 20)* around each of next 2 sts on row below last, fpdc around each skipped st, sk next 4 sts on last row, sc in next 4 sts, sk next 6 sts on row before last from last fpdc; rep from * 9 times more; fpdc around each of next 2 sts on last row below, fpdc around each skipped st, sk next 4 sts on last row, sc in next 2 sts, turn.

Row 5: Ch 1, sc in first 2 sts; *fpdc around next 2 post sts on row below last, sk next 2 sts on last row, sc in next 2 sts, fpdc around next 4 post sts on row below last, sk next 4 sts on last row, sc in next 2 sts, fpdc around next 2 post sts on row below last, sk next 2 sts on last row, sc in next 4 sts; rep from * 8 times more, *fpdc around next 2 post sts on row below last, sk next 2 sts on last row, sc in next 2 sts, fpdc around next 4 post sts on row below last, sk next 4 sts on last row, sc in next 2 sts, fpdc around next 2 post sts on row below last, sk next 2 sts on last row, sc in last 2 sts, turn.

Row 7: Ch 1, sc in first 2 sts, *fpdc around each of next 2 post sts on row before last, sk next 2 sts on last row, sc in next 2 sts, __cable__ *(see Special Stitches on page 20),* sk next 4 sts on last row, sc in next 2 sts, fpdc around next 2 post sts on row before last, sk next 2 sts on last row, sc in next 4 sts; rep from * 8 times more, fpdc around each of next 2 post sts on row before last, sk next 2 sts on last row, sc in next 2 sts, cable, sk next 4 sts on last row, sc in next 2 sts, fpdc around next 2 post sts on row before last, sk next 2 sts on last row, sc in last 2 sts, turn.

Row 9: Ch 1, sc in first 2 sts, *fpdc around next 2 post sts on row before last, sk next 2 sts on last row, sc in next 2 sts, fpdc around next 4 post sts on row before last, sk next 4 sts on last row, sc in next 2 sts, fpdc around next 2 post sts on row before last, sk next 2 sts on last row, sc in next 4 sts; rep from * 8 times more, fpdc around next 2 post sts on

row before last, sk next 2 sts on last row, sc in next 2 sts, fpdc around next 4 post sts on row before last, sk next 4 sts on last row, sc in next 2 sts, fpdc around next 2 post sts on row before last, sk next 2 sts on last row, sc in last 2 sts, turn.

Row 11: Ch 1, sc in first 2 sts, *fpdc around next 2 post sts on row before last, sc in next 2 sts, cable, sk next 4 sts on last row, sc in next 2 sts, fpdc around next 2 post sts on row before last, sk next 2 sts on last row, sc in next 4 sts; rep from * 8 times more; fpdc around next 2 post sts on row before last, sc in next 2 sts, cable, sk next 4 sts on last row, sc in next 2 sts, fpdc around next 2 post sts on row before last, sk next 2 sts on last row, sc in last 2 sts, turn.

Row 12: Ch 1, sc in each st across, turn.

Rows 13–20: [Rep Rows 11 and 12] 4 times.

Row 21: Ch 1, sc in first 2 sts, cable, *sk next 4 sts on last row, sc in next 4 sts, cable; rep from * 8 times more, sk next 4 sts on last row, sc in last 2 sts, turn.

Row 23: Ch 1, sc in first 2 sts, fpdc around next 4 post sts on row before last, sk next 4 sts on last row; *sc in next 4 sts, fpdc around next 4 post sts on row before last, sk next 4 sts on last row; rep from * 8 times more, sc in last 2 sts, turn.

Row 25: Ch 1, sc in first 2 sts, cable, sk next 4 sts on last row, *sc in next 4 sts, cable, sk next 4 sts on last row; rep from * 8 times more, sc in last 2 sts, turn.

Row 26: Ch 1, sc in each st across, turn.

[Rep Rows 5–26] 5 times.

Rep Rows 5–21. Fasten off.

Continued on page 27

Diamond Strips

A basic single crochet stitch is all that is needed to crochet strips in a solid color, or in black and white stripes.

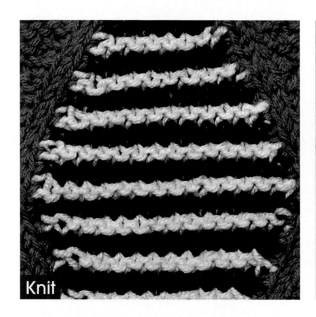
Knit

Crochet

Crochet Stitch Pattern

Row 1: With larger hook, loosely ch 3, sc in 2nd ch from hook and in next ch, turn. *(2 sc)*

Row 2 & all even-numbered rows: Ch 1, sc in each sc, turn.

Row 3: Ch 1, 2 sc in each sc, turn. *(4 sc)*

Row 5: Ch 1, 2 sc in first st, sc in next 2 sc, 2 sc in next sc, turn. *(6 sc)*

Row 7: Ch 1, 2 sc in first sc, sc in each sc to last sc, 2 sc in last sc, turn. *(8 sc)*

Row 9: Rep Row 7. *(10 sc)*

Row 11: Rep Row 7. *(12 sc)*

Row 13: Rep Row 7. *(14 sc)*

Row 15: Rep Row 7. *(16 sc)*

Note: *For **sc dec**: pull up lp in each of next 2 sc, yo and draw through all 3 lps on hook.*

Row 17: Ch 1, **sc dec** *(see Note)* over first 2 sc, sc in each sc to last 2 sc, sc dec over last 2 sc, turn. *(14 sc)*

Row 19: Rep Row 17. *(12 sc)*

Row 21: Rep Row 17. *(10 sc)*

Row 23: Rep Row 17. *(8 sc)*

Row 25: Rep Row 17. *(6 sc)*

Row 27: Rep Row 17. *(4 sc)*

Row 29: Ch 1, sc dec 2 times, turn. *(2 sc)*

Row 30: Ch 1, sc in each sc.

Rep Rows 3–30 for pattern.

Diamond Strips Afghan

Design by Darla Sims

*Fashioned in bright grenadine and dramatic black-and-white stripes,
this afghan has a retro flower-power look. Accents of loopy flowers created on
a flower loom add a whimsical note to this a cheerful bedroom addition.*

■■■□ INTERMEDIATE

Finished Size
Approximately 53 x 72 inches

Materials
Coats & Clark Red Heart Classic medium (worsted) weight yarn:
    45 oz/3150 yds/1350g
    #730 grenadine (A)
    21 oz/1470 yds/630g #1 white (B)
    14 oz/980 yds/420g #12 black (C)
Sizes H/8/5mm and I/9/5.5mm crochet hooks or sizes needed to obtain gauge
Yarn needle
4-inch diameter flower loom

4 MEDIUM

Gauge
7 sc = 2 inches

Strip A (make 8)
Row 1: With larger hook and A, loosely ch 3, sc in 2nd ch from hook and in next ch, turn. *(2 sc)*

Row 2 & all even-numbered rows: Ch 1, sc in each sc, turn.

Row 3: Ch 1, 2 sc in each sc, turn. *(4 sc)*

Row 5: Ch 1, 2 sc in first st, sc in next 2 sc, 2 sc in next sc, turn. *(6 sc)*

Row 7: Ch 1, 2 sc in first sc, sc in each sc to last sc, 2 sc in last sc, turn. *(8 sc)*

Row 9: Rep Row 7. *(10 sc)*

Row 11: Rep Row 7. *(12 sc)*

Row 13: Rep Row 7. *(14 sc)*

Row 15: Rep Row 7. *(16 sc)*

Note: *For **sc dec**: pull up lp in each of next 2 sc, yo and draw through all 3 lps on hook.*

Row 17: Ch 1, **sc dec** *(see Note)* over first 2 sc, sc in each sc to last 2 sc, sc dec over last 2 sc, turn. *(14 sc)*

Row 19: Rep Row 17. *(12 sc)*

Row 21: Rep Row 17. *(10 sc)*

Row 23: Rep Row 17. *(8 sc)*

Row 25: Rep Row 17. *(6 sc)*

Row 27: Rep Row 17. *(4 sc)*

Row 29: Ch 1, sc dec 2 times, turn. *(2 sc)*

Row 30: Ch 1, sc in each sc, turn.

[Rep Rows 3–30] 8 times.

Last row: Ch 1, sc dec.
Fasten off.

Strip B (make 7)

Row 1: With larger hook and C, loosely ch 3, sc in 2nd ch from hook and in next ch, turn. *(2 sc)*

Rows 2–30: Rep Rows 2–30 of Strip A, working 2 rows of C and 2 rows of B. [Rep Rows 3–30] 7 times more.

Last row: Ch 1, sc dec. Fasten off.

Strip Edging

With smaller hook and A, join yarn in sc of last row of 1 strip, ch 1, sc in same sc and in next sc, working along edge of strip, sc in each row and 2 sc in each point row to beg ch; working across point end in unused lps of beg ch, sc in each lp; working along next edge of strip, sc in each row and 2 sc in each point row to first sc; join with sl st in first sc. Fasten off.
Rep on rem strips.

Flowers (make 63)

With B and making a figure 8, wind yarn 3 times around matching pegs on flower loom, pull yarn to back and cut, leaving a 3-inch tail. Thread C into yarn needle. Working close to center of flower, wrap yarn in between each petal 3 times, pull yarn to back of work. Knot all ends tog.

Assembly

Beg and ending with a Strip A and alternating rem strips, with A, sl st strips tog through back lps only.

Border

*Note: For **3-sc dec:** draw up lp in each of 3 sts or sps indicated, yo and draw through all 4 lps on hook.*

Hold afghan with RS facing you and 1 short end at top, with smaller hook, join A in first sc at top of first strip, ch 1, sc in same st, *3 sc in next sc, sc in each sc to first sc of next 3-sc group, **3-sc dec** *(see Note)* over first sc, joining and first sc on next strip; sc in each sc to first sc at top of point, sc in first sc; rep from * 6 times more; working across next side, sc in each sc and 3 sc in first sc of each point to next side; working in same manner, work across rem sides; join with sl st in first sc. Fasten off.

Finishing

Referring to photo for placement, sew flowers to afghan. ♣

Entwined Cables Afghan

Continued from 23

Edging

Rnd 1: With smaller hook, join A in any corner, ch 1, sc in same st as joining, sc around working 3 sc in each outer corner; join with sl st in first sc.

Rnd 2: Ch 3 (counts as dc), dc in each sc and 3 dc in center sc of each corner, join with sl st in 3rd ch of beg ch-3.. Fasten off.

Rnd 3: Attach B in center dc of any corner, ch 3, dc in next 6 dc, *cl *(see Special Stitch on page 22)*, dc in next 7 dc; rep from * around, join with sl st in 3rd ch of beg ch-3. Fasten off.

Rnd 4: Rep Rnd 2 with A. Fasten off. ♣

Bobbled Diamonds

*Popcorns, single crochet stitches and post stitches
are the ingredients of this textured stitch pattern.*

Knit

Crochet

Crochet Stitch Pattern

Special Stitches

For **front post double crochet (fpdc)**, yo,
insert hook from front to back around post
(see Stitch Guide) of st indicated, yo, draw lp
through, [yo, draw through 2 lps on hook]
2 times.

For **back post double crochet (bpdc)**,
Yo, insert hook from back to front around
post *(see Stitch Guide)* of st indicated on row
below last, yo, pull up lp to height of working row, [yo, draw through 2 lps on hook]
2 times.

For **popcorn (pc)**, 5 dc in st indicated,
remove lp from hook, insert hook in first dc,
draw dropped lp through.

Multiple of 14 sts + 18

Row 1 (RS): Ch 32, sc in 2nd ch from hook
and in each ch across, turn. *(31 sc)*

Row 2 & all even-numbered rows: Ch 1,
sc in each st across, turn.

Row 3: Ch 1, sc in first 6 sts, sk first 6 sts
on row before last, **fpdc** *(see Special Stitches)*
around each of next 2 sts; sk next 2 sts on
last row, **pc** *(see Special Stitches)* in next st, sk
next st on row before last, fpdc around each
of next 2 sts, sk next 2 sts on last row, sc in
next 9 sts, sk next 9 sts on row before last,
fpdc around each of next 2 sts, sk next 2 sts
on last row, pc in next st, sk next st on row
before last, fpdc around each of next 2 sts,
sk next 2 sts on last row, sc in last 6 sts, turn.

Row 5: Ch 1, sc in first 5 sts, fpdc around next 2 fpdc on row before last, sk next 2 sts on last row, sc in next 3 sts, fpdc around next 2 fpdc on row before last, sk next 2 sts on last row, sc in next 7 sts, fpdc around next 2 fpdc on row before last, sk next 2 sts on last row, sc in next 3 sts, fpdc around next 2 fpdc on row before last, sk next 2 sts on last row, sc in last 5 sts, turn.

Row 7: Ch 1, sc in first 4 sts, [fpdc around next 2 fpdc on row before last, sk next 2 sts on last row, sc in next 5 sts] 3 times, fpdc around next 2 fpdc on row before last, sk next 2 sts on last row, sc in last 4 sts, turn.

Row 9: Ch 1, sc in first 3 sts, *fpdc around next 2 fpdc on row before last, sk next 2 sts on last row, sc in next 7 sts, fpdc around next 2 fpdc on row before last, sk next 2 sts on last row, sc in next 3 sts; rep from * once more, turn.

Row 11: Ch 1, sc in first st, pc in next st, fpdc around next 2 fpdc on row before last, sk next 2 sts on last row, sc in next 9 sts, fpdc around next 2 fpdc on row before last, sk next 2 sts on last row, pc in next st, fpdc around next 2 fpdc on row before last, sk next 2 sts on last row, sc in next 9 sts, fpdc around next 2 fpdc on row before last, sk next 2 sts on last row, pc in next st, sc in last st, turn.

Row 13: Rep Row 9.

Row 15: Rep Row 7.

Row 17: Rep Row 5.

Row 18: Ch 1, sc in each st across, turn.

Rep Rows 3–18 for pattern.

Bobbled Diamonds Throw

Design by Darla Sims

Soft and cuddly in a light and airy bouclé yarn, this textural beauty will be the afghan everyone loves. Its classic styling will never go out of fashion.

 INTERMEDIATE

Finished Size
Approximately 46 x 57 inches

Materials
Red Heart TLC Amore medium (worsted) weight yarn:

4 MEDIUM

48 oz/2320 yds/1360g #3625 celery
Sizes H/8/5mm and I/9/5.5mm crochet hooks or sizes needed to obtain gauge

Gauge
With larger hook:
6 sts = 2 inches; 8 rows = 2 inches

Row 1 (RS): With larger hook, ch 144, sc in 2nd ch from hook and in each ch across, turn. *(143 sc)*

Row 2 & all even-numbered rows: Ch 1, sc in each st across, turn.

Row 3: Ch 1, sc in first 6 sts, sk first 6 sts on row before last, ***fpdc** (see Special Stitches on page 28) around each of next 2 sts on row before last, sk next 2 sts on last row, **pc** (see Special Stitches on page 28) in next st, sk next st on row before last, fpdc around each of next 2 sts; sk next 2 sts on last row, sc in next 9 sts; rep from * 8 times; fpdc around each of next 2 sts on row before last; sk next 2 sts on last row, pc in next st, sk next st on row before last, fpdc around each of next 2 sts, sk next 2 sts on last row, sc in last 6 sts, turn.

Row 5: Ch 1, sc in first 5 sts; *fpdc around next 2 fpdc on row before last, sk next 2 sts on last row, sc in next 3 sts, fpdc around next 2 fpdc, sk next 2 sts on last row, sc in next 7 sts; rep from * 7 times more; fpdc around next 2 fpdc on row before last, sk next 2 sts on last row, sc in next 3 sts, fpdc around next 2 fpdc, sk next 2 sts on last row, sc in last 5 sts, turn.

Row 7: Ch 1, sc in first 4 sc; *fpdc around next 2 fpdc on row before last, sk next 2 sts on last row, sc in next 5 sts, fpdc around next 2 fpdc on row before last, sk next 2 sts on last row, sc in next 5 sts; rep from * 7 times more; fpdc around next 2 fpdc on row before last, sk next 2 sts on last row, sc in next 5 sts, fpdc around next 2 fpdc on row before last, sk next 2 sts on last row, sc in last 4 sts, turn.

Row 9: Ch 1, sc in first 3 sts; *fpdc around next 2 fpdc on row before last, sk next 2 sts on last row, sc in next 7 sts, fpdc around next 2 fpdc on row before last, sc in next 3 sc; rep from * across, turn.

Row 11: Ch 1, sc in first st; *pc in next st, fpdc around next 2 fpdc on row before last, sk next 2 sts on last row, sc in next 9 sts, fpdc around next 2 fpdc on row before last, sk next 2 sts on last row; rep from * 7 times more; pc in next st, sc in last st, turn.

Row 13: Rep Row 9.

Row 15: Rep Row 7.

Row 17: Rep Row 5.

Row 18: Ch 1, sc in each st across, turn.

Rep Rows 3–18 until afghan measures approximately 56 inches, ending with Row 3. Fasten off.

Border

Rnd 1: With smaller hook, join yarn in first st in upper right-hand corner, ch 1, 3 sc in same st; sc in each sc to last st, 3 sc in last st; working along next side, sc evenly across to next corner; working across next side, 3 sc in first st; sc in each st to last st, 3 sc in last st; working across next side, sc evenly across to first sc; join with sl st in first sc.

Rnd 2: Ch 3 *(counts as a dc)*, work [fpdc, **bpdc,** *{see Special Stitches on page 28},* fpdc] around next sc, *bpdc around next sc, fpdc around next sc; rep from * to 2nd sc of next corner; work [fpdc, bpdc, fpdc] around next sc; **bpdc around next sc, fpdc around next sc; rep from ** to 2nd sc of next corner; work [fpdc, bpdc, fpdc] around next sc; ***bpdc around next sc, fpdc around next sc; rep from *** to 2nd sc of next corner; work [fpdc, bpdc, fpdc] around next sc; ****bpdc around next sc, fpdc around next sc; rep from **** to beg ch-3; join with sl st in 3rd ch of beg ch-3.

Rnd 3: Ch 3, bpdc around each bpdc, fpdc around each fpdc, and work [fpdc, bpdc, fpdc] around bpdc of each corner; join with sl st in 3rd ch of beg ch-3.

Rnd 4: Rep Rnd 3. Fasten off. ❖

Zigzag Chevron

*The ups and downs of this stitch pattern resembles a knitted ripple design; it is
recreated here with front post double crochet stitches that alternate with single crochet stitches.*

Knit

Crochet

Crochet Stitch Pattern

Special Stitch

For **front post double crochet (fpdc)**, yo,
insert hook from front to back around post
(see Stitch Guide) of st indicated, yo, draw lp
through, [yo, draw through 2 lps on hook]
2 times.

Multiple of 20 sts + 1

Row 1: Ch 21, sc in 2nd ch from hook,
sc each ch across, turn. *(20 sc)*

Row 2 & all even-numbered rows: Ch 1,
sc in each st across, turn.

Row 3: Ch 1, sc in first 2 sts, sk first 2 sts
on row before last, **fpdc** *(see Special Stitch)*
around next 7 sts on row before last, sc in

next 3 sts on last row, fpdc around each of
next 7 sts on row before last, sc in last 2 sts
on last row, turn.

Row 5: Ch 1, sc in first 3 sts, sk first 3 sts
on row before last, fpdc around next 5 post
sts on row before last, sc in next 5 sts, fpdc
around next 5 post sts, sc in last 3 sts, turn.

Row 7: Ch 1, sc in first 4 sts, sk first 4 sts on
row before last, fpdc around next 3 post sts,
sc in next 7 sts, fpdc around next 3 post sts,
sc in last 4 sts, turn.

Row 9: Ch 1, fpdc around first st on row before
last, sk first st on last row, [sc in next 4 sts on last
row, sk next 4 sts on row below last, fpdc around
next st on row before last] 4 times, turn.

Row 11: Ch 1, fpdc around first 2 sts on row before last, sk first 2 sc on last row sc in next 7 sts, fpdc around next 3 sts, sc in next 7 sts, fpdc around last 2 sts, turn.

Row 13: Ch 1, fpdc around first 3 sts on row before last, sk first 3 sts on last row, sc in next 5 sts, fpdc around next 5 sts, sc in next 5 sts, fpdc around last 3 sts, turn.

Row 15: Ch 1, fpdc around first 4 sts, sk first 4 sts on last row, sc in next 3 sts on last row, fpdc around next 7 sts on row before last, sk

next 7 sts on last row, sc in next 3 sts on last row, fpdc around last 4 sts, turn.

Row 17: Ch 1, sc in first st, [fpdc around next 4 sts, sc in next st] 4 times, turn.

Row 19: Ch 1, sc in first 2 sts, fpdc around next 7 sts, sc in next 3 sts, fpdc around next 7 sts, sc in last 2 sts on last row, turn.

Row 20: Ch 1, sc in each st across, turn.

Rep Rows 5–20 for pattern.

Zigzag Chevron Throw

Design by Donna Jones

*This is the kind of afghan that soothes the soul and warms your toes.
You'll enjoy watching the zigzag pattern appear as you crochet.*

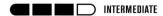 INTERMEDIATE

Finished Size
Approximately 45 x 55 inches, without fringe

Materials
Patons Canadiana medium (worsted) weight yarn:
   45 oz/2925 yds/1350g #152 sand
Size J/10/6mm crochet hook or size needed to obtain gauge

4 MEDIUM

Gauge
5 sts = 2 inches; 6 rows = 2 inches in pattern

Row 1: Ch 112, sc in 2nd ch from hook, sc each ch across, turn. *(111 sc)*

Row 2 & all even-numbered rows: Ch 1, sc in each st across, turn.

Row 3: Ch 1, sc in first 2 sts, **fpdc** *(see Special Stitch on page 32)* around next 7 sts on row before last, *sc in next 3 sts on last

row, fpdc around each of next 7 sts on row before last; rep from * 9 times more, sc in last 2 sts on last row, turn.

Row 5: Ch 1, sc in first 3 sts, fpdc around next 5 sts on row before last, *sc in next 5 sts, fpdc around next 5 sts; rep from * 9 times more, sc in last 3 sts, turn.

Row 7: Ch 1, sc in first 4 sts, fpdc around next 3 sts, *sc in next 7 sts, fpdc around next 3 sts; rep from * 9 times more, sc in last 4 sts, turn.

Row 9: Ch 1, fpdc around first st, *sc in next 4 sts, fpdc around next st on row before last; rep from * across, turn.

Row 11: Ch 1, fpdc around first 2 sts, sc in next 7 sts, *fpdc around next 3 sts, sc in next 7 sts; rep from * 9 times more, fpdc around last 2 sts, turn.

Row 13: Ch 1, fpdc around first 3 sts, sc in next 5 sts, *fpdc around next 5 sts, sc in next

5 sts; rep from * 9 times more, fpdc around last 3 sts, turn.

Row 15: Ch 1, fpdc around first 4 sts, sc in next 3 sts, *fpdc around next 7 sts, sc in next 3 sts; rep from * 9 times more, fpdc around last 4 sts, turn.

Row 17: Ch 1, sc in first st, *fpdc around next 4 sts, sc in next st; rep from * across, turn.

Row 19: Ch 1, sc in first 2 sts, fpdc around next 7 sts, *sc in next 3 sts, fpdc around next 7 sts; rep from * 9 times more, sc in last 2 sts on last row, turn.

Row 20: Ch 1, sc in each st across, turn.

Rep Rows 5–20 until piece measures about 55 inches long, ending with Row 9.

Last row: Ch 1, sc in each st.
Fasten off.

Fringe

For each **knot,** cut 3 strands yarn each 9 inches long. Holding all strands tog as 1, fold in half; insert crochet hook from back to front through st, pull fold through st, pull ends through fold, pull snug.

Knot fringe in every 2nd st across short ends. Trim ends even. ❖

Ripple Ridges

*Front post single and double crochet stitches combine
to form the ridges on this stunning pattern.*

Knit

Crochet

Crochet Stitch Pattern

Special Stitches

For **cluster (cl)**, keeping last lp of each dc on hook, dc in 3 sts indicated, yo, draw through 4 lps on hook.

For **small cluster (sm cl)**, keeping last lp of each dc on hook, dc in st indicated, sk next st, dc in next st, yo, draw through 3 lps on hook.

For **front post single crochet (fpsc)**, yo, insert hook from front to back around post *(see Stitch Guide)* of st indicated, yo, draw lp through, yo, draw through 2 lps on hook.

For **front post double crochet (fpdc)**, yo, insert hook from front to back around post *(see Stitch Guide)* of st indicated, yo, draw lp through, (yo, draw through 2 lps on hook) twice.

Multiple of 18 sts + 20

Pattern Note

Pattern stitch is worked in 2 colors.

*Note: For **dc dec**, [yo, insert hook in next st, yo, draw lp through, yo, draw through 2 lps on hook] 2 times; yo, draw through 3 lps on hook.*

Row 1: With A, ch 20, dc in 3rd ch from hook, dc in next 7 chs, 3 dc in next ch, dc in next 7 chs, **cl** *(see Special Stitches)* over next 3 chs, dc in next 7 chs, 3 dc in next ch, dc in 7 chs, **dc dec** *(see Note)* over last 2 chs, turn. Fasten off. *(37 sts)*

Row 2: With WS of Row 1 facing you, join B with sc in first st, **fpsc** *(see Special Stitches)* around next 17 sts, sk next st, fpsc around next 17 sts, sc in last st. Fasten off. *(37 sts)*

Row 3: Hold piece with opposite side of beg ch at top, with WS of Row 1 facing you, join A with sc in unused lp of first ch, ch 2 *(counts as first dc)*, dc in same lp, working in rem unused lps, dc in next 7 lps; **sm cl** *(see Special Stitches on page 36)* over next 3 lps, dc in next 7 lps, (dc, ch 1, dc) in next lp, dc in next 7 lps, sm cl over next 3 lps, dc in next 6 chs, 2 dc in last ch, turn. Fasten off. *(36 sts)*

Row 4: Join other color with sc in first st, fpsc around each st across to next ch-1 sp, ch 2, sk ch-1 sp, fpsc around each st across to last st, sc in last st, turn.

Row 5: Ch 1, 2 sc in first st, fpsc in next 8 sts, sk next st, fpsc around each of next 8 sts, working into ch sps of last 2 rows as 1, (sc, ch 1, sc) in next ch sp, fpsc around each of next 8 sts on last row, sk next st, fpsc around each of next 8 sts, 2 sc in last st, turn. *(38 sts)*

Row 6: (Sc, ch 2, dc) in first st, **fpdc** *(see Special Stitches on page 36)* around each of next 7 sts; skipping 2 sts between dc, sm cl over next 4 sts, fpdc around next 7 sts, (dc, ch 1, dc) in next ch-1 sp, fpdc around next 7 sts; skipping 2 sts between dc, sm cl over next 4 sts, fpdc in next 7 sts, 2 dc in last st, turn. *(36 sts)*

Row 7: (Sc, ch 2, dc) in first st, dc in next 7 sts, cl, dc in next 7 sts, (dc, ch 1, dc) in next ch-1 sp, dc in next 7 sts, cl, dc in next 7 sts, 2 dc in last st, turn. Fasten off.

Rep Rows 4–7 for desired length alternating A and B, ending with a Row 7 in A.

Last row: With RS of last row facing you, join B with sc in first st, fpsc around next 8 sts, sk next st, fpsc around next 8 sts, sc in next ch-1 sp, fpsc around next 8 sts, sk next st, fpsc around next 8 sts, sc in last st. Fasten off.

Ripple Ridges Throw

Design by Donna Jones

Choose one variegated worsted weight yarn and a matching solid color, and you have all that is needed for this ripple afghan. This pattern features raised ridges for added dimension and an up-to-date look.

◨◼◼◻ **INTERMEDIATE**

Finished Size
Approximately 44 x 58 inches, not including fringe

Materials
Patons Décor medium (worsted) weight yarn:
    28 oz/1960 yds/840g
        #1641 periwinkle (A)
    28 oz/1960 yds/840g
        #16240 Newport ombre (B)
Size I/9/5.5mm hook or size hook needed to obtain gauge

4 MEDIUM

Gauge
8 sts = 2 inches; 8 rows in pattern = 3 inches; point to point in pattern = 4 inches
   *Note: For **dc dec**, [yo, insert hook in next st, yo, draw lp through, yo, draw through 2 lps on hook] 2 times; yo, draw through 3 lps on hook.*

Row 1: With A, ch 200, dc in 3rd ch from hook, dc in next 7 chs, 3 dc in next ch, *dc in next 7 chs, **cl** *(see Special Stitches on page 36)* over next 3 chs, dc in next 7 chs, 3 dc in next ch; rep from * 9 more times, dc in 7 chs, **dc dec** *(see Note)* over last 2 chs, turn. Fasten off. *(199 sts)*

Row 2: With WS of Row 1 facing you, join B with sc in first st, **fpsc** *(see Special Stitches on page 36)* around each of next 17 sts, *sk next st, fpsc around next 17 sts; rep from * 9 times more, sc in last st. Fasten off. *(189 sts)*

Row 3: Hold piece with opposite side of beg ch at top, with WS of Row 1 facing you, join A with sc in unused lp of first ch, ch 2 *(counts as first dc),* dc in same lp, working in rem unused lps, dc in next 7 lps; **sm cl** *(see Special Stitches on page 36)* over next 3 lps, *dc in next 7 lps, (dc, ch 1, dc) in next lp, dc in next 7 lps, sm cl over next 3 lps; rep from * 9 times more, dc in next 6 chs, 2 dc in last ch, turn. Fasten off. *(189 sts, 10 ch sps)*

Row 4: Join other color with sc in first st, *fpsc around each st across to next ch-1 sp, ch 2, sk ch-1 sp; rep from * 9 times more, fpsc around each st across to last st, sc in last st, turn.

Row 5: Ch 1, 2 sc in first st, fpsc in next 8 sts, sk next st, *fpsc around each of next 8 sts, working into ch sps of last 2 rows as 1, (sc, ch 1, sc) in next ch sp, fpsc around each of next 8 sts on last row, sk next st; rep from * 8 times more, fpsc around each of next 8 sts, 2 sc in last st, turn. *(200 sts, 10 ch-1 sps)*

Row 6: (Sc, ch 2, dc) in first st, **fpdc** *(see Special Stitches on page 36)* around each of

next 7 sts; skipping 2 sts between dc, sm cl over next 4 sts, *fpdc around next 7 sts, (dc, ch 1, dc) in next ch-1 sp, fpdc around next 7 sts; skipping 2 sts between dc, sm cl over next 4 sts; rep from * 9 times more, fpdc in next 7 sts, 2 dc in last st, turn. *(189 sts, 10 ch sps)*

Row 7: (Sc, ch 2, dc) in first st, dc in next 7 sts, cl, *dc in next 7 sts, (dc, ch 1, dc) in next ch-1 sp, dc in next 7 sts, cl; rep from * 9 times more, dc in next 7 sts, 2 dc in last st, turn. Fasten off.

Rows 8–291: Rep Rows 4–7 alternating colors, ending with Row 7 in B.

Last row: With RS of last row facing you, join B with sc in first st, fpsc around next 8 sts, sk next st, fpsc around next 8 sts, *sc in next ch-1 sp, fpsc around next 8 sts, sk next st, fpsc around next 8 sts; rep from * to last st, sc in last st. Fasten off.

Fringe

For each **knot,** cut 4 strands B each 8 inches long. Holding all strands tog as one, fold in half, insert hook from back to front through st, pull fold through st, pull ends through fold, pull snug.

Knot fringe in each corner, in each point and at base of each "V" across first and last rows. Trim ends even. ❧

Rambling Blackberries & Seed Stitch

Traditionally only seen in knitted patterns, the Rambling Blackberry motif is created with front post double crochet stitches and popcorn stitches. The crocheted version of the Seed Stitch is simply a combination of single crochet and chain stitches.

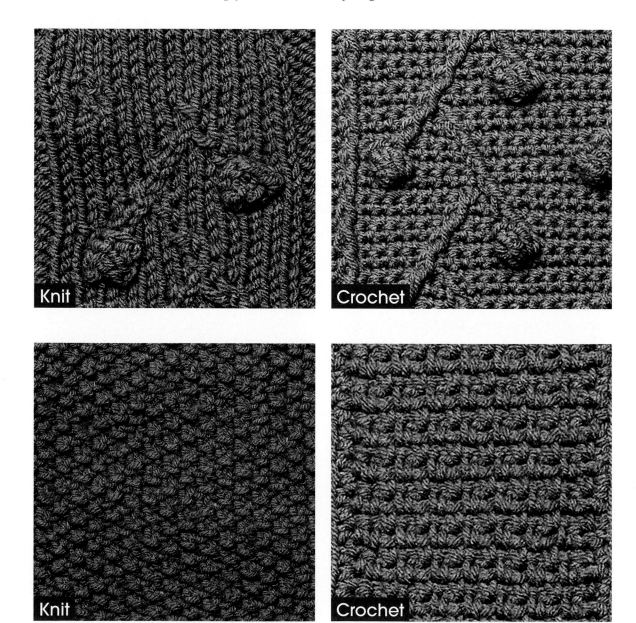

Knit

Crochet

Knit

Crochet

Crochet Stitch Pattern

Special Stitches

For **front post double crochet (fpdc)**, yo, insert hook from front to back around post *(see Stitch Guide)* of st indicated, yo, draw lp through, (yo, draw through 2 lps on hook) 2 times.

For **popcorn (pc)**, 5 dc in st indicated, remove lp from hook, insert hook in first dc, draw dropped lp through.

Rambling Blackberry

Multiple of 13 sts + 1

Row 1 (RS): With larger hook, loosely ch 14, sc in 2nd ch from hook and in each ch across, turn. *(13 sc)*

Row 2 & all even-numbered rows: Ch 1, sc in each st, turn.

Row 3: Ch 1, sc in first 2 sts, sk first 2 sts on row before last, **fpdc** *(see Special Stitches)* around next sc on row before last, sk next st on last row, [sc in next 3 sts, sk next st on row before last from fpdc, fpdc around next st, sk next st on last row, sc in next 2 sts, sk next 4 sts on row before last from last fpdc, fpdc around next st, sk next st on last row, sc in next 6 sts] 2 times, fpdc around next st on row before last, sk next st on last row, sc in last 2 sts, turn.

Row 5: Ch 1, sc in first 2 sts, fpdc around next fpdc, sk next st on last row, [sc in next 4 sts, fpdc around each of next 2 fpdc, sk next 2 sts on last row, sc in next 7 sts] 2 times, fpdc around next fpdc, sk next st on last row, sc in last 2 sts, turn.

Row 7: Ch 1, sc in first 2 sts, fpdc around next fpdc, sk next st on last row, [sc in next 5 sts, fpdc around first fpdc on row before last, sk next st on row before last, sc in next 4 sts, **pc** *(see Special Stitches)* in next st, sc in

next 2 sts] 2 times, fpdc around next fpdc, sk next st on last row, sc in last 2 sts, turn.

Row 9: Ch 1, sc in first 2 sts, fpdc around next fpdc, sk next st on last row, [sc in next 6 sts, fpdc around fpdc on row before last, sk next st on last row, sc in next 2 sts, fpdc around top of pc, sk next st on last row, sc in next 3 sts] 2 times, fpdc around next fpdc, sk next st on last row, sc in last 2 sts, turn.

Row 11: Ch 1, sc in first 2 sts, fpdc around next fpdc, sk next st on last row, [sc in next 7 sts, fpdc around each of next 2 post sts, sk next 2 sts on last row, sc in next 4 sts] 2 times, fpdc around next fpdc, sk next st on last row, sc in last 2 sts, turn.

Row 13: Ch 1, sc in first 2 sts, fpdc around next fpdc, sk next st on last row, [sc in next 2 sts, pc in next st, sc in next 4 sts, fpdc around 2nd fpdc on row before last, sk next st on last row, sc in next 5 sts] 2 times, fpdc around next fpdc, sk next st on last row, sc in last 2 sts turn.

Row 15: Ch 1, sc in first 2 sts, fpdc around next fpdc, sk next st on last row, [sc in next 3 sts, fpdc around top of pc, sk next st on last row, sc in next 2 sts, fpdc around next fpdc, sk next st on last row, sc in next 6 sts] 2 times, fpdc around next fpdc, sk next st on last row, sc in last 2 sts, turn.

Row 16: Ch 1, sc in each st, turn.

Rep Rows 5–16 for pattern.

Seed Stitch

Multiple 16 sts + 1

Row 1: With larger hook, loosely ch 16, sc in 2nd ch from hook, *ch 1, sk next ch, sc in next ch; rep from * across, turn.

Row 2: Ch 1, sc in first sc and in next ch-1 sp, *ch 1, sc in next ch-1 sp; rep from * to last sc, sc in last sc, turn.

Row 3: Ch 1, sc in first sc, *ch 1, sc in next ch-1 sp; rep from * across.

Rep Rows 2 and 3 for pattern.

Rambling Blackberries Afghan

Design by Darla Sims

We've combined Seed Stitch with Rambling Blackberry in panels for a harmonious afghan design. Try it in a shade that is in harmony with your decorating style.

 **INTERMEDIATE**

Finished Size
Approximately 51 x 58 inches

Materials
Coats & Clark Red Heart TLC Essentials medium (worsted) weight yarn:
   54 oz/2934 yds/1530g
   #2348 purple mist
Sizes I/9/5.5mm and J/10/6mm crochet hooks or sizes needed to obtain gauge
Yarn needle

4 MEDIUM

Gauge
In Seed Stitch pattern: panel = 4 inches wide
In Rambling Blackberry pattern: panel = 11 inches wide

Rambling Blackberry Panel (make 3)
Row 1 (RS): With larger hook, loosely ch 33, sc in 2nd ch from hook and in each ch across, turn. *(32 sc)*

Row 2 & all even-numbered rows: Ch 1, sc in each st, turn.

Row 3: Ch 1, sc in first 2 sts, sk first 2 sts on row before last, **fpdc** *(see Special Stitches on page 41)* around next st on row before last, sk next st on last row, [sc in next 3 sts, sk next st on row before last from fpdc, fpdc around next st, sk next st on last row, sc in next 2

sts, sk next 4 sts on row before last from last fpdc, fpdc around next st, sk next st on last row, sc in next 6 sts] 2 times, fpdc around next st on row before last, sk next st on last row, sc in last 2 sts, turn.

Row 5: Ch 1, sc in first 2 sts, fpdc around next fpdc, sk next st on last row, [sc in next 4 sts, fpdc around each of next 2 fpdc, sk next 2 sts on last row, sc in next 7 sts] 2 times, fpdc around next fpdc, sk next st on last row, sc in last 2 sts, turn.

Row 7: Ch 1, sc in first 2 sts, fpdc around next fpdc, sk next st on last row, [sc in next 5 sts, fpdc around first fpdc on row before last, sk next st on last row, sc in next 4 sts, **pc** *(see Special Stitches On page 41)* in next st, sc in next 2 sts] 2 times, fpdc around next fpdc, sk next st on last row, sc in last 2 sts, turn.

Row 9: Ch 1, sc in first 2 sts, fpdc around next fpdc, sk next st on last row, [sc in next 6 sts, fpdc around fpdc on row before last, sk next st on last row, sc in next 2 sts, fpdc around top of pc, sk next st on last row, sc in next 3 sts] 2 times, fpdc around next fpdc, sk next st on last row, sc in last 2 sts, turn.

Row 11: Ch 1, sc in first 2 sts, fpdc around next fpdc, sk next st on last row, [sc in next 7 sts, fpdc around each of next 2 fdpc, sk next 2 sts on last row, sc in next 4 sts] 2 times, fpdc around next fpdc, sk next st on last row, sc in last 2 sts, turn.

Row 13: Ch 1, sc in first 2 sts, fpdc around next fdpc, sk next st on last row, [sc in next 2 sts, pc in next st, sc in next 4 sts, fpdc around 2nd fpdc on row before last, sk next sc on last row, sc in next 5 sts] 2 times; fpdc around next fpdc, sk next st on last row, sc in last 2 sts, turn.

Row 15: Ch 1, sc in first 2 sts, fpdc around next fpdc, sk next st on last row, [sc in next 3 sts, fpdc around top of pc, sk next st on last row, sc in next 2 sts, fpdc around next fpdc, sk next st on last row, sc in next 6 sts] 2 times, fpdc around next fpdc, sk next st on last row, sc in last 2 sts, turn.

Row 16: Ch 1, sc in each st.
[Rep Rows 5–16] 14 times.
Rep Rows 5–11.
Fasten off.

Seed Stitch Panel (make 4)
Row 1: With larger hook, loosely ch 16, sc in 2nd ch from hook, *ch 1, sk next ch, sc in next ch; rep from * across, turn.

Row 2: Ch 1, sc in first sc and in next ch-1 sp, *ch 1, sc in next ch-1 sp; rep from * to last sc, sc in last sc, turn.

Row 3: Ch 1, sc in first sc, *ch 1, sc in next ch-1 sp; rep from * across.

Rep Rows 2 and 3 until panel measures approximately 55 inches long or same length as Rambling Blackberry panel. Fasten off.

Edging
With smaller hook, sc around each panel, working 3 sc in each corner; join with a sl st in first sc. Fasten off.

Assembly
Working through back lps only of sc on each panel, sew panels tog, beg and ending with a Seed Stitch panel and alternating rem panels.

Border
Rnd 1: With smaller hook and RS facing, join yarn in 2nd sc of any corner, ch 1, 3 sc in same sc, sc in each sc around, working 3 sc in each corner; join with a sl st in first sc.

Rnds 2 & 3: Ch 1, sc in same st as joining, sc in each sc and 3 sc in 2nd sc of each corner around; join in first sc.

Rnd 4: Ch 3 *(counts as a dc)*, 4 dc in same sc as joining, remove hook and insert in 3rd ch of beg ch-3 and 4th dc, yo, draw lp through for beg pc, sc in next 5 sc, *pc in next sc, sc in next 5 sc; rep from * around, adjusting last rep as necessary; join with a sl st top of beg pc. Fasten off. ✤

Chapter 3
Home Accents

Whether you want a quick gift to crochet or just want to try a new stitch while making something for your home, here's an enticing array of projects.

Floral Trellis

A single crochet background is used with front post and crossed front post stitches to form the trellis design.

Knit

Crochet

Crochet Stitch Pattern

Special Stitches

To **hook yarn,** wrap yarn clockwise around hook. ***Note:*** *A regular yarn over is wrapped counterclockwise.*

For **backward sc (bsc),** with wrong side of work facing you, holding hook behind yarn, insert hook from back to front through next st, **hook yarn** *(see above),* pull through st, yo, pull through 2 lps on hook.

For **front post double crochet (fpdc),** yo, insert hook from front to back around post *(see Stitch Guide)* of st indicated, yo, draw lp through, [yo, draw through 2 lps on hook] 2 times.

For **crossed front post double crochet (x-fpdc),** sk next fpdc, fpdc *(see above)* around next fpdc; working in front of last st made, fpdc around skipped fpdc.

Note: *Sk 2 sts on last row behind x-fpdc.*

Multiple of 10 sts + 13

Row 1 (RS): Ch 23, sc in 2nd ch from hook and in each ch across, turn. *(22 sc)*

Row 2 & all even-numbered rows: Ch 1, **bsc,** *(see Special Stitches)* in each ch across, turn.

Row 3: Ch 1, sc in first 4 sts, **fpdc** *(see Special Stitches)* around 6th sc on row before last, sk next st on last row, sc in next 2 sts, fpdc around next st on row before last, sk next st on last row, sc in next 6 sts, sk next 8 sts on row before last, fpdc around next st, sk next st on last row, sc in next 2 sts, fpdc around next st on row before last, sk next st on last row, sc in next 4 sts, turn.

Row 5: Ch 1, sc in first 3 sts, fpdc around first fpdc on row before last, [sk next st on last row, sc in next 4 sts, fpdc around next fpdc on row before last] 3 times, sc in next 3 sts, turn.

Row 7: Ch 1, sc in first 2 sts, fpdc around first fpdc, sk next st on last row, sc in next 6 sts, fpdc around next fpdc, sk next st on last row, sc in next 2 sts, fpdc around next fpdc, sk next st on last row, sc in next 6 sts, fpdc around next fpdc, sk next st on last row, sc in next 2 sts, turn.

Row 9: Ch 1, sc in first sc, fpdc around first fpdc, sk next st on last row, sc in next 8 sts, fpdc around each of next 2 fpdc, sk next 2 sts on last row, sc in next 8 sc, fpdc around next fpdc, sk next st on last row, sc in next st, turn.

Row 11: Ch 1, for **first x-fpdc,** fpdc around first fpdc, fpdc around first st on row before last, sk first 2 sts on last row, sc in next 8 sc, **x-fpdc** *(see Special Stitches on page 46),* sk next 2 sts on last row, sc in next 8 sc, for **last x-fpdc,** sk next fpdc, fpdc around last sc on row before last; pull up lp in last st on last row, yo, pull up lp around skipped fpdc, yo, draw through 2 lps on hook, yo, draw through all 3 lps on hook, turn.

Row 13: Ch 1, sc in first 2 sts, sk first fpdc, fpdc around next fpdc, sk next st on last row, sc in next 6 sts, fpdc around first fpdc of next x-fpdc *(behind),* sk next st on last row, sc in next 2 sts, fpdc around next fpdc of same x-fpdc *(in front),* sk next sc on last row, sc in next 6 sc, fpdc around next fpdc, sc in next 2 sts, turn.

Row 15: Ch 1, sc in first 3 sts, fpdc around first fpdc, [sk next st on last row, sc in next 4 sts, fpdc around next fpdc] 3 times, sk next st on last row, sc in next 3 sts, turn.

Row 17: Ch 1, sc in first 4 sc, fpdc around first fpdc, sk next st on last row, sc in next 2 sts, fpdc around next fpdc, sk next st on last row, sc in next 6 sts, fpdc around next fpdc, sk next st on last row, sc in next 2 sts, fpdc around next fpdc, sk next st on last row, sc in next 4 sts, turn.

Row 19: Ch 1, sc in first 5 sts, fpdc around each of next 2 fpdc, sk next 2 sts on last row, sc in next 8 sts, fpdc around each of next 2 fpdc, sk next 2 sts on last row, sc in next 5 sts, turn.

Row 21: Ch 1, sc in first 5 sc, x-fpdc, sk next 2 sts on last row, sc in next 8 sts, x-fpdc, sk next 2 sts, sc in next 5 sts, turn.

Row 23: Ch 1, sc in first 4 sts, fpdc around first fpdc of x-fpdc *(behind),* sk next st on last row, sc in next 2 sts, fpdc around 2nd fpdc of same x-fpdc *(in front),* sk next st on last row, sc in next 6 sts, fpdc around first fpdc of next x-fpdc, sk next st on last row, sc in next 2 sts, fpdc around 2nd fpdc of same x-fpdc, sk next st on last row, sc in next 4 sts, turn.

Row 24: Ch 1, bsc in each st across, turn.

Rep Rows 5–24 for pattern.

Floral Trellis Pillow

Design by Donna Jones

Definitely for the garden lover, this pillow adds a light and flowery touch to sofa, chair or bed. Flowers and vines are added with sport weight yarn after assembling the pillow.

 **EASY**

Finished Size
14½ inches square

Materials
Coats & Clark Red Heart Super Saver medium (worsted) weight yarn:
    8 oz/560 yds/224g
        #316 soft white (A)
    J.&P. Coats Luster Sheen fine (sport) weight yarn:
        2 oz #206 crystal pink (B)
        1 oz #227 buttercup (C)
        2 oz #673 aqua (D)
    Size D/3/3.25mm crochet hook (for floral trims)
    Size H/8/5mm crochet hook or hook size needed to obtain gauge
    14 x 14-inch pillow form—purchased or sewn *(see Pattern Note)*
    Optional (for sewn pillow form)
        ½ yd lightweight fabric
        Matching sewing thread
        Sewing machine or needle
        Polyester fiberfill

Gauge
With medium weight yarn and larger hook: 7 sc = 2 inches; 8 rows = 2 inches

Pattern Note
For **sewn** pillow form, before beginning assembly, using crochet front as pattern, cut 2 pieces of lightweight fabric each ½ inch larger on each edge than crocheted Front. With right sides together, matching edges, sew together ¼ inch from each edge leaving an 8-inch opening for turning. Turn right sides out, stuff with fiberfill, sew opening closed. Pillow form should be slightly larger than crocheted Front.

Front
Row 1 (RS): With larger hook and A, ch 53, sc in 2nd ch from hook and in each ch across, turn. *(52 sc made)*

Row 2 & all even-numbered rows: Ch 1, **bsc,** *(see Special Stitches on page 46)* in each ch across, turn.

Row 3: Ch 1, sc in first 4 sts, **fpdc** *(Special Stitches on page 46)* around 6th sc on row before last, sk next st on last row, sc in next 2 sts, fpdc around next st on row before last, [sk next st on last row, sc in next 6 sts, sk next 8 sts on row before last, fpdc around next st, sk next st on last row, sc in next 2 sts, fpdc around next st on row before last] 4 times, sk next st on last row, sc in next 4 sts, turn.

Row 5: Ch 1, sc in first 3 sts, fpdc around first fpdc on row before last, [sk next st on last row, sc in next 4 sts, fpdc around next fpdc on row before last] across to last 3 sts, sc in next 3 sts, turn.

Row 7: Ch 1, sc in first 2 sts, fpdc around first fpdc, sk next st on last row, sc in next 6 sts, fpdc around next fpdc, [sk next st on last row, sc in next 2 sts, fpdc around next fpdc, sk next st on last row, sc in next 6 sts, fpdc around next fpdc] 4 times, sk next st on last row, sc in last 2 sts, turn.

Row 9: Ch 1, sc in first sc, fpdc around first fpdc, sk next st on last row, sc in next 8 sts, [fpdc around each of next 2 fpdc, sk next 2 sts on last row, sc in next 8 sc] 4 times, fpdc around next fpdc, sk next st on last row, sc in next st, turn.

Row 11: Ch 1, for **first x-fpdc,** fpdc around first fpdc, fpdc around first st on row before last, sk first 2 sts on last row, sc in next 8 sc, [**x-fpdc** (*see Special Stitches on page 46),* sk next 2 sts on last row, sc in next 8 sc] 4 times, for **last x-fpdc,** sk next fpdc, fpdc around last sc on row before last; pull up lp in last st on last row, yo, pull up lp around skipped fpdc, yo, draw through 2 lps on hook, yo, draw through all 3 lps on hook, turn.

Row 13: Ch 1, sc in first 2 sts, sk first fpdc, fpdc around next fpdc, sk next st on last row, sc in next 6 sts, [fpdc around first fpdc of next x-fpdc *(behind),* sk next st on last row, sc in next 2 sts, fpdc around 2nd fpdc of same x-fpdc *(in front),* sk next sc on last row, sc in next 6 sc] 4 times, fpdc around next fpdc, sc in next 2 sts, turn.

Row 15: Ch 1, sc in first 3 sts, fpdc around first fpdc, [sk next st on last row, sc in next 4 sts, fpdc around next fpdc] 9 times, sk next st on last row, sc in next 3 sts, turn.

Row 17: Ch 1, sc in first 4 sc, fpdc around first fpdc, sk next st on last row, sc in next 2 sts, fpdc around next fpdc, [sk next st on last row, sc in next 6 sts, fpdc around next fpdc, sk next st on last row, sc in next 2 sts, fpdc around next fpdc] 4 times, sk next st on last row, sc in next 4 sts, turn.

Row 19: Ch 1, sc in first 5 sts, fpdc around each of next 2 fpdc, sk next 2 sts on last row, [sc in next 8 sts, fpdc around each of next 2 fpdc] 4 times, sk next 2 sts on last row, sc in next 5 sts, turn.

Row 21: Ch 1, sc in first 5 sc, x-fpdc, [sk next 2 sts on last row, sc in next 8 sts, x-fpdc] 4 times, sk next 2 sts, sc in next 5 sts, turn.

Row 23: Ch 1, sc in first 4 sts, fpdc around first fpdc of x-fpdc (*behind*), sk next st on last row, sc in next 2 sts, fpdc around 2nd fpdc of same x-fpdc (*in front*), [sk next st on last row, sc in next 6 sts, fpdc around first fpdc of next x-fpdc, sk next st on last row, sc in next 2 sts, fpdc around 2nd fpdc of same x-fpdc] 4 times, sk next st on last row, sc in next 4 sts, turn.

Row 24: Ch 1, bsc in each st across, turn.

Back
Row 1 (RS): With A, ch 50, dc in 4th ch from hook *(beg 3 skipped chs count as a dc)* and in each ch across, turn. *(48 sts)*

Row 2: Ch 3, dc in each st, turn.

Rep Row 2 until back is same size as front. Fasten off.

Assembly & Edging
*Note: For **sc dec**, pull up lp in each of next 2 sts indicated, yo and draw through all 3 lps on hook.*

Rnd 1: Hold front and back WS tog with edges matching. Working through both layers as 1, ch 1; working around all edges, sc in each st and in end of each row around with 3 sc at each corner, inserting pillow form before closing last edge, join with sl st in first sc.

Rnd 2: Ch 1, sc in each st around, join.

Rnd 3: Ch 1, sc in each st around with **sc dec** *(see Note)* at each corner, join. Fasten off.

Fold Rnd 3 to Rnd 1, forming a tube with WS of sc on outside. Sew sc on Rnd 3 to base of sts on Rnd 1.

Floral Trim
Flower (make 7)
Rnd 1: With smaller hook and C, ch 2, sl st in 2nd ch from hook to form ring, ch 1, 7 sc in ring, join with sl st in first sc. Fasten off.

Rnd 2: With smaller hook and B, join with a sc in any st, (ch 1, 3 dc, ch 1) in same st as joining sc, (sc, ch 1, 3 dc, ch 1) in each st around, join in first sc. Fasten off, leaving an end for sewing.

Bud (make 7)
Row 1 (RS): For **stem** and **calyx,** with smaller hook and D, ch 15, 3 sc in 2nd ch from hook, turn.

Row 2: Ch 1, sc in each st across, changing to B in last sc, turn.

Row 3: For **petals,** working in **back lps** only *(see Stitch Guide)* of Row 2, sl st in first st, ch 1, (hdc, 3 dc, hdc) in next st, ch 1, sl st in next st, working in rem lps of Row 2, (ch 1, hdc, ch 1, dc, ch 1, hdc, ch 1) in first st, sl st in next st, (ch 1, hdc, ch 1, dc, ch 1, hdc, ch 1) in next st, join with sl st in first sl st. Fasten off, leaving an end for sewing.

Leaf (make 9)
*Note: For **picot,** ch 3, sl st in last st made.*

Rnd 1: With smaller hook and D, ch 6, sk first ch from hook *(mark this ch),* sc in next 4 chs, (sc, ch 1, sc *{mark this sc},* ch 1, sc) in last ch, working on opposite side in unused lps of beg ch, (hdc, **picot** *{see Note}*) in next ch, dc in next ch, (dc, picot) in next ch, dc in next ch, (dc, picot, 3 dc, picot, 3 dc, picot, dc) in marked ch. **Do not join.**

Rnd 2: (Dc, picot) in next st, dc in next st, (dc, picot) in next st, hdc in next st, sc in next st, ch 1, sk next st, sl st in next ch, ch 15 for **stem.** Fasten off, leaving an end for sewing.

Finishing
Referring to photo, arrange flowers, buds and leaves as desired on front of pillow. Sew edges in place weaving stems over and around front post sts to resemble vines. ❧

Diamonds & Lace

While in knitting yarn overs and slipped stitches form a lacy pattern, in this lacy crochet version chain stitches and double crochet stitches create the holes.

Knit

Crochet

Crochet Stitch Pattern

Special Stitches

For **beginning dc (beg dc),** (sc, ch 2) in first st.

For **filet dc (fdc),** yo, insert hook through center of st under top 3 strands, complete as dc.

For **ending dc (end dc),** skip next ch, dc in next ch.

Multiple of 16 sts + 22

Row 1 (RS): Ch 38, **beg dc** *(see Special Stitches)* in 2nd ch from hook, dc in next 7 chs, [ch 1, sk next ch, dc in next ch] 3 times, dc in next 10 chs, [ch 1, sk next ch, dc in next ch] 3 times, dc in next 7 chs, turn. *(37 sts and chs)*

Row 2: Beg dc, **fdc** *(see Special Stitches)* in next st, ch 1, sk next st, fdc in next 5 sts,

[ch 1, sk next ch, fdc in next st] 3 times, fdc in next 4 sts, ch 1, sk next st, fdc in next 5 sts, [ch 1, sk next ch, fdc in next st] 3 times, fdc in next 4 sts, ch 1, sk next st, fdc in next st, **end dc** *(see Special Stitches),* turn.

Row 3: Beg dc, ch 1, sk next st, dc in next ch-1 sp, ch 1, sk next st, fdc in next 4 sts, [ch 1, sk next ch, fdc in next st] 3 times, fdc in next 3 sts, ch 1, sk next st, dc in next ch-1 sp, ch 1, sk next st, fdc in next 4 sts, [ch 1, sk next ch, fdc in next st] 3 times, fdc in next 3 sts, ch 1, sk next st, dc in next ch-1 sp, ch 1, sk next st, end dc, turn.

Row 4: Beg dc, dc in next ch-1 sp, ch 1, sk next st, dc in next ch-1 sp, fdc in next 4 sts, [ch 1, sk next ch, fdc in next st] 3 times, fdc

in next 3 sts, dc in next ch-1 sp, ch 1, sk next st, dc in next ch-1 sp, fdc in next 4 sts; [ch 1, sk next ch, fdc in next st] 3 times, fdc in next 3 sts, dc in next ch-1 sp, ch 1, sk next st, dc in next ch-1 sp, end dc, turn.

Row 5: Beg dc, fdc in next st, dc in next ch-1 sp, fdc in next 5 sts, [ch 1, sk next ch, fdc in next st] 3 times, fdc in next 4 sts, dc in next ch-1 sp, fdc in next 5 sts, [ch 1, sk next ch,

dc in next st] 3 times, fdc in next 4 sts, dc in next ch-1 sp, fdc in next dc end dc, turn.

Rows 6 & 7: Beg dc, fdc in next 7 sts, [ch 1, sk next ch, fdc in next st] 3 times, dc in next 10 sts [ch 1, sk next ch, dc in next st] 3 times, dc in next 6 sts, end dc, turn.

Rep Rows 2–7 for pattern, ending last rep with a Row 6. Fasten off.

Diamonds & Lace Pillow

Design by Donna Jones

The interesting shape and vibrant color of a hand-crafted neck-roll pillow is uniquely suited to a bedroom or living-room sofa.

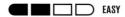 **EASY**

Finished Size
9 inches across x 14 inches long, not including tassels

Materials
Bernat Berella "4" medium (worsted) weight yarn:

4 MEDIUM

    7 oz/490 yds/196g #8826 peach
Size I/9/5.5mm crochet hook or size hook needed to obtain gauge
9-inch diameter x 14-inch long neck-roll pillow form—purchased or sewn *(see Pattern Notes)*
5-inch square of cardboard (for tassel)
Optional (for sewn pillow form)
    ½ yd lightweight fabric
    Matching sewing thread
    Sewing machine or needle
    Polyester fiberfill

Gauge
7 fdc = 2 inches; 7 fdc rows = 3 inches

Pattern Notes
For **sewn** pillow form, before beginning assembly, using crochet side and ends as

patterns, cut 1 piece lightweight fabric each ½ inch larger on each edge than each of the crochet pieces. Mark center of each end. With right sides together, matching edges and allowing ¼ inch for seams, sew short edges of pillow together across 1 inch at each end, forming a tube and leaving a 12-inch opening for turning. Easing to fit, sew 1 round end piece to each end of tube. Turn right sides out, stuff with fiberfill. Sewn pillow side should be slightly larger than crocheted Side piece.

For **purchased or sewn** pillow form, run 28-inch strand of yarn through center of pillow form; leaving 7-inch tails extended, secure tails at center of each pillow end.

Sew opening closed on sewn pillow form.

Pillow End (make 2)
Rnd 1: Ch 4, sl st in first ch to form ring, ch 3 *(counts as first dc)*, 11 dc in ring, join with sl st in top of ch-3. *(12 dc made)*

Rnd 2: (Ch 3, dc) in first st, 2 dc in each st around, join. *(24 sts)*

Rnd 3: (Ch 3, dc) in first st, dc in next st, [2 dc in next st, dc in next st] 11 times, join. *(36 sts)*

Rnd 4: Ch 3, dc in next st, [2 dc in next st, dc in next 2 sts] 11 times, 2 dc in next st, join. *(48 sts)*

Rnd 5: (Ch 3, dc) in first st, dc in next 3 sts, [2 dc in next st, dc in next 3 sts] 11 times, join. *(60 sts)*

Rnd 6: Ch 3, dc in next st, 2 dc in next st, [dc in next 4 sts, 2 dc in next st] 11 times, dc in next 2 sts, join. *(72 sts)*

Rnd 7: (Ch 3, dc) in first st, dc in next 5 sts, [2 dc in next st, dc in next 5 sts] 11 times, join. *(84 sts)*

Rnd 8: Ch 3, dc in next 2 sts, 2 dc in next st, [dc in next 6 sts, 2 dc in next st] 11 times, dc in next 3 sts, join. *(96 sts)*

Rnd 9: Working from left to right, **reverse sc** *(see Stitch Guide)* in each st around, join with sl st in first st.
Fasten off.

Pillow Side

Row 1 (RS): Ch 54, **beg dc** *(see Special Stitches on page 52)* in 2nd ch from hook, dc in next 7 chs, *[ch 1, sk next ch, dc in next ch] 3 times, dc in next 10 chs; rep from * once, [ch 1, sk next ch, dc in next ch] 3 times, dc in next 7 chs, turn. *(37 sts and chs made)*

Row 2: Beg dc, **fdc** *(see Special Stitches on page 52)* in next st, ch 1, sk next st, fdc in next 5 sts, *[ch 1, sk next ch, fdc in next st] 3 times, fdc in next 4 sts, ch 1, sk next st, fdc in next 5 sts; rep from * once, [ch 1, sk next ch, fdc in next st] 3 times, fdc in next 4 sts, ch 1, sk next st, fdc in next st, **end dc** *(see Special Stitches on page 52),* turn.

Row 3: Beg dc, ch 1, sk next st, dc in next ch-1 sp, ch 1, sk next st, fdc in next 4 sts, *[ch 1, sk next ch, fdc in next st] 3 times, fdc in next 3 sts, ch 1, sk next st, dc in next ch-1 sp, ch 1, sk next st, fdc in next 4 sts; rep from * once more, [ch 1, sk next ch, fdc in next st] 3 times, fdc in next 3 sts, ch 1, sk next st, dc in next ch-1 sp, ch 1, sk next st, end dc, turn.

Row 4: Beg dc, dc in next ch-1 sp, ch 1, sk next st, dc in next ch-1 sp, fdc in next 4 sts, *[ch 1, sk next ch, fdc in next st] 3 times, fdc in next 3 sts, dc in next ch-1 sp, ch 1, sk next st, dc in next ch-1 sp, fdc in next 4 sts; rep from * once more, [ch 1, sk next ch, fdc in next st] 3 times, fdc in next 3 sts, dc in next ch-1 sp, ch 1, sk next st, dc in next ch-1 sp, end dc, turn.

Row 5: Beg dc, fdc in next st, dc in next ch-1 sp, fdc in next 5 sts, *[ch 1, sk next ch, fdc in next st] 3 times, fdc in next 4 sts, dc in next ch-1 sp, fdc in next 5 sts; rep from * once more, [ch 1, sk next ch, dc in next st] 3 times, fdc in next 4 sts, dc in next ch-1 sp, fdc in next dc, end dc, turn.

Rows 6 & 7: Beg dc, fdc in next 7 sts, *[ch 1, sk next ch, fdc in next st] 3 times, dc in next 10 sts; rep from * once, [ch 1, sk next ch, dc in next st] 3 times, dc in next 6 sts, end dc, turn.

Rows 8–55: [Rep Rows 2–7] 8 times.

Rows 56–60: Rep Rows 2–6.
Fasten off.

Assembly

With RS facing, sew last row to beg ch on Row 1 across eight sts at each end, forming a tube and leaving an opening for turning. Easing to fit and leaving Rnd 9 extended, sew tops of sts on Rnd 8 *(beside sts of Rnd 9)* of 1 end piece to each end of tube. Turn RS out, insert pillow form, sew opening closed. On each end, pull 7-inch tails through ring of Rnd 1.

Continued on page 59

Flying Geese

Create this distinctive pattern with backward single crochets for the background.
The raised geese are formed with a clever use of chain stitches.

Knit

Crochet

Crochet Stitch Pattern

Special Stitches

To **hook yarn,** wrap yarn clockwise around hook. ***Note:*** *A regular yarn over (yo) is wrapped counterclockwise.*

For **backward sc (bsc),** with WS of work facing you and holding hook behind yarn, insert hook from back to front through next st, **hook yarn** *(see above),* draw through st, yo, draw through 2 lps on hook.

For **sc ch-7 and next st tog**, insert hook under ch-7 and through next st on last row, complete as sc.

Multiple of 10 sts + 12

Row 1 (RS): Beg at top, ch 22, sc in 2nd ch from hook and in each ch across, turn. *(21 sc)*

Row 2: Ch 1, **bsc,** *(see Special Stitches)* in each st, turn.

Row 3: Ch 1, sc in first 3 sts, ch 7, sk next 5 sts, sc in next 5 sts, ch 7, sk next 5 sts, sc in next 3 sts, turn.

Row 4: Ch 1, bsc in first 3 sts, working in front of ch-7, hdc in next 5 sts on row below, bsc in next 5 sts, working in front of ch-7, hdc in next 5 sts, bsc in next 3 sts, turn.

Row 5: Ch 1, sc in first 5 sts, **sc ch-7 and next st tog,** *(see Special Stitches),* sc in next 9 sts, sc ch-7 and next st tog, sc in next 5 sts, turn.

Row 6: Ch 1, bsc in each st across, turn.

Row 7: Ch 1, sc in first 8 sts, ch 7, sk next 5 sts, sc in next 8 sts, turn.

Row 8: Ch 1, bsc in first 8 sts, working in front of ch-7, hdc in next 5 sts on row below, bsc in next 8 sts, turn.

Row 9: Ch 1, sc in first 10 sts, sc ch-7 and next st tog, sc in next 10 sts, turn.

Row 10: Ch 1, bsc in each st across, turn.

Rep Rows 3–10 for pattern.

Flying Geese Rectangular Pillow

Design by Donna Jones

Whether you need a pillow to prop up a book or to rest your head, this design will fit in with any decorating style.

 EASY

Finished Size
12½ x 16½ inches, not including fringe

Materials
Bernat Berella "4" medium (worsted) weight yarn:
    7 oz/350 yds/196g #8923 burgundy
Size G/6/4mm crochet hook or hook size needed to obtain gauge
12 x 16-inch pillow form—purchased or sewn *(see Pattern Note)*
    Optional (for sewn pillow form)
      ½ yd lightweight fabric
      Matching sewing thread
      Sewing machine or needle
      Polyester fiberfill

4 MEDIUM

Pattern Note
For sewn pillow form, before beginning assembly, using crochet front as pattern, cut 2 pieces lightweight fabric each ½ inch larger on each edge than front. With right sides together, matching edges, sew together ¼ inch from each edge leaving an 8-inch opening for turning. Turn right sides out, stuff with fiberfill, sew opening closed. Sewn pillow form should be slightly larger than crocheted Front).

Gauge
4 sc = 1 inch; 9 rows = 2 inches

Front
Row 1 (RS): Beg at top, ch 62, sc in 2nd ch from hook and in each ch across, turn. *(61 sts)*

Row 2: Ch 1, **bsc,** *(see Special Stitches on page 56)* in each st, turn.

Row 3: Ch 1, sc in first 3 sts, [ch 7, sk next 5 sts, sc in next 5 sts] 5 times, ch 7, sk next 5 sts, sc in next 3 sts, turn.

Row 4: Ch 1, bsc in first 3 sts, [working in front of ch-7, hdc in next 5 sts on row below, bsc in next 5 sts] 5 times, working in front of ch-7, hdc in next 5 sts, bsc in next 3 sts, turn.

Row 5: Ch 1, sc in first 5 sts, **sc ch-7 and next st tog,** *(see Special Stitches on page 56),* [sc in next 9 sts, sc ch-7 and next st tog] 5 times, sc in next 5 sts, turn.

Row 6: Ch 1, bsc in each st across, turn.

Row 7: Ch 1, sc in first 8 sts, [ch 7, sk next 5 sts, sc in next 5 sts] 5 times, sc in next 3 sts, turn.

Row 8: Ch 1, bsc in first 8 sts, [working in front of ch-7, hdc in next 5 sts on row below, bsc in next 5 sts] 5 times, sc in next 3 sts, turn.

Row 9: Ch 1, sc in first 10 sts, sc ch-7 and

next st tog, [sc in next 9 sts, sc ch-7 and next st tog] 4 times, sc in next 10 sts, turn.

Row 10: Ch 1, bsc in each st across, turn.

Rows 11–50: [Rep Rows 3–10] 5 times.

Row 51: Ch 1, sc in each st across. Fasten off.

Back
Row 1 (RS): Ch 62, sc in 2nd ch from hook and in each rem ch, turn. *(61 sts)*

Row 2: Ch 2 *(counts as first hdc)*, hdc in each st across, turn.

Row 3: Ch 1, sc in each st across.

Rep Rows 2 and 3 until same size as front.

Assembly
If using sewn pillow form *(see Pattern Note)*, make now.
Hold front and back with WS tog and edges matching. Working through both layers as one, join with sc in any corner; working around all edges, sc in each st and in end of each row around with 2 sc at each corner, inserting pillow form before closing, join with sl st in first st. Fasten off.

Fringe
For **fringe**, cut 5-inch strands yarn. For each knot, hold 2 strands tog as 1 and fold in half; insert hook from back to front through st, pull fold through st, pull ends through fold, pull snug. Place knot at each corner and in every other st across both short edges of pillow. Trim ends even. ❖

Diamond & Lace Pillow
Continued from 55

Tassels (make 2)
For **tassel,** cut 2 (18-inch) strands yarn, fold 1 strand in half, lay both strands aside. Wrap yarn 30 times around 5-inch cardboard. Remove cardboard and run folded strand through lps; tie tightly. Tightly wrap other 18-inch strand 5 times around lps 1 inch below first knot; tie tightly and run all ends back through tassel to hide. Cut lps, trim ends even to 3½ inches past last wraps. Using 7-inch tails, tie one tassel to center of each end, run tails back through tassels to hide. ❖

Long Stitch

This easy yet effective pattern is formed with long single crochet stitches over a single crochet and backward single crochet background.

Knit

Crochet

Crochet Stitch Pattern

Special Stitches

To **hook yarn,** wrap yarn clockwise around hook ***Note:*** *A regular yarn over (yo) is wrapped counterclockwise.*

For **backward single crochet (bsc),** with WS of work facing you, holding hook behind yarn, insert hook from back to front through next st, **hook yarn** *(see above),* draw through st, yo, draw through 2 lps on hook.

For **long single crochet (long sc),** insert hook in indicated st on 4th row below, pull up to height of working row, complete as for sc. ***Note:*** *Sk st behind long sc on last row.*

Multiple of 6 sts + 10

Row 1 (RS): Ch 16, sc in 2nd ch from hook and in each ch across, turn. *(15 sc)*

Row 2 & all even-numbered rows: Ch 1, **bsc** *(see Special Stitches)* in each sc, turn.

Row 3: Ch 1, sc in each st, turn.

Row 5: Ch 1, sc in first st, **long sc** *(see Special Stitches)* in 2nd st on 4th row below, *sc in next 5 sts on last row, sk next 5 sts on 4th row below, long sc in next st; rep from * once more, sc in next st on last row, turn.

Row 7: Ch 1, sc in each st, turn.

Row 9: Ch 1, sc in first 4 sts, long sc in 5th st on 4th row below, sc in next 5 sts on last row, sk next 5 sts on 4th row below, long sc in next st, sc in next 4 sts on last row, turn.

Rep Rows 2–9 for pattern.

Long-Stitch Square Pillow

Design by Donna Jones

This pillow is made in straight rows but is assembled by bringing all four corners to the back.
This makes it look like you crocheted on the diagonal.

 **EASY**

Finished Size
12 inches square, not including tassels

Materials
Bernat Berella "4" medium (worsted) weight yarn:
    7 oz/490 yds/200g #8799 light eggplant
5-inch square piece of cardboard
Size G/6/4mm crochet hook or hook size needed to obtain gauge
12-inch square pillow form—purchased or sewn *(see Pattern Note)*
    Optional (for sewn pillow form)
      ½ yd lightweight fabric
      Matching sewing thread
      Sewing machine or needle
      Polyester fiberfill

Gauge
4 sc = 1 inch; 4 rows = 1 inch

Pattern Note
For **sewn** pillow form, before beginning assembly, using folded crochet piece as pattern, cut 2 pieces lightweight fabric each ½ inch larger on each edge than folded piece. With right sides together, matching edges, sew together ¼ inch from each edge leaving an 8-inch opening for turning. Turn right sides out, stuff with fiberfill, sew opening closed. Sewn pillow form should be slightly larger crocheted Front.

Pillow
Row 1: Ch 64, sc in 2nd ch from hook and in each ch across, turn. *(63 sc)*

Row 2 & all even-numbered rows: Ch 1, **bsc** *(see Special Stitches on page 60)* in each st, turn.

Row 3: Ch 1, sc in each st, turn.

Row 5: Ch 1, sc in first st, **long sc** *(see Special Stitches on page 60)* in 2nd st on 4th row below, *sc in next 5 sts on last row, sk next 5 sts on 4th row below, long sc in next st; rep from * to last st, sc in next st on last row, turn.

Row 7: Ch 1, sc in each st, turn.

Row 9: Ch 1, sc in first 4 sts, long sc in 5th st on 4th row below, *sc in next 5 sts on last row, sk next 5 sts on 4th row below, long sc in next st; rep from * to last 4 sts, sc in last 4 sts on last row, turn.

Rep Rows 2–9 until piece measures the same in length and width. Fasten off.

Assembly
With WS facing, fold as shown in Fig 1.

Continued on page 75

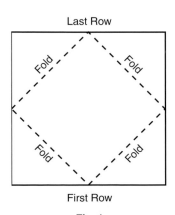

Fig. 1

Woven Effect

The crocheted version of this basket-weave or woven-look pattern is attained by working in the front posts where there would have been knit stitches and in the back posts for the purl stitches.

Knit

Crochet

Crochet Stitch Pattern

Special Stitches

For **front post double crochet (fpdc)**, yo, insert hook from front to back around post (*see Stitch Guide*) of st indicated, yo, draw lp through, [yo, draw through 2 lps on hook] 2 times.

For **back post double crochet (bpdc)**, yo, insert hook from back to front around post (*see Stitch Guide*) of st indicated, yo, draw lp through, [yo, draw through 2 lps on hook] 2 times.

Multiple of 12 sts + 2

Row 1: Ch 16, dc in 4th ch from hook

(beg 3 skipped chs counts as a dc) and in each ch across, turn. *(14 dc)*

Rows 2–4: Ch 2 *(counts as first hdc)*, **fpdc** *(see Special Stitches)* around each of next 6 sts, **bpdc** *(see Special Stitches)* around each of next 6 sts, hdc in last st, turn.

Rows 5–8: Ch 2, bpdc around each of next 6 sts, fpdc around each of next 6 sts, hdc in last st, turn.

Rows 9–12: Ch 2, fpdc around each of next 6 sts, bpdc around each of next 6 sts, hdc in last st, turn.

Rep Rows 5–12 for pattern.

Woven-Effect Rug

Design by Donna Jones

A refreshing change of pace from the usual purchased throw rug, you can add this interesting accessory to your home environment.

◼◼◻◻ **EASY**

Finished Size
Approximately 22 x 33 inches

Materials
Coats & Clark Red Heart Grandé super bulky (super chunky) weight yarn:
36 oz/895 yds/1080g
#2672 light thyme
Size K/10½/6.5mm crochet hook or size hook needed to obtain gauge

6 **SUPER BULKY**

Gauge
6 sts = 2¼ inches; 4 rows = 2¼ inches

Center
Row 1 (RS): Ch 88, dc in 4th ch from hook *(beg 3 skipped chs counts as a dc)* and in each ch across, turn. *(86 sts)*

Rows 2–4: Ch 2 *(counts as first hdc)*, ***fpdc** *(see Special Stitches on page 63)* around each of next 6 sts, **bpdc** *(see Special Stitches on page 63)* around each of next 6 sts; rep from * 6 times more, hdc in last st, turn.

Rows 5–8: Ch 2, *bpdc around each of next 6 sts, fpdc around each of next 6 sts; rep from * 6 times more, hdc in last st, turn.

Rows 9–12: Ch 2, *fpdc around each of next 6 sts, bpdc around each of next 6 sts; rep from * 6 times more, hdc in last st, turn.

[Rep Rows 5–12] 3 times.

At end of last row, **do not fasten off.**

Border
Rnd 1: Working around outer edge of center, *sc in each st across, ch 1, work 56 sc evenly spaced across ends of rows to next corner, ch 1; rep from * once, join with sl st in first sc. *(284 sc and 4 ch-1 sps)*

Rnd 2: Ch 1, sc in **back lp** only *(see Stitch Guide)* of same sc, sc in **front lp** only *(see Stitch Guide)* of next sc; *(sc in back lp only of next st, sc in front lp only of next st) to corner ch-1 sp, (sc, ch 1, sc) in ch-1 sp; rep from * 3 times more, join in first sc.

Rnd 3: Ch 1, sc in front lp only of same sc, *(sc in back lp only of next sc, sc in front lp only of next sc) to corner ch-1 sp, (sc, ch 1, sc) in ch-1 sp; rep from * 3 times more, sc in back lp only of next sc; join in first sc.

Row 4: Ch 1, sc in back lp only of same sc, sc in front lp only of next sc, *(sc in back lp only of next st, sc in front lp only of next st) to corner ch-1 sp, (sc, ch 1, sc) in ch-1 sp; rep from * 3 times more, sc in back lp only of next st, sc in front lp only of next sc, join in first sc. Fasten off. ❖

Striped Zigzag

The stripes in this pattern are simply long single crochets worked into the previous rows. Subtle zigzags are evident in this ripple style design.

Knit

Crochet

Crochet Stitch Pattern

Special Stitches

To **hook yarn,** wrap yarn clockwise around hook. ***Note:*** *A regular yarn over (yo) is wrapped counterclockwise.*

For **backward sc (bsc),** with wrong side of work facing you and holding hook behind yarn, insert hook from back to front through next st, **hook yarn** *(see above),* draw through st, yo, draw through 2 lps on hook.

For **long single crochet (long sc),** insert hook in indicated st on row before last, pull up to height of working row, complete as sc.

Multiple 13 sts + 15

Note: *For **sc dec**, pull up lp in each of next 2 sts indicated, yo and draw through all 3 lps on hook.*

Row 1 (RS): With 2 strands yarn held tog, ch 28, 2 sc in 2nd ch from hook, sc in next 4 chs, sk next 2 chs, **sc dec** *(see Note)* over next 2 chs, sc in next 4 chs, (sc, ch 1, sc) in next ch; sc in next 4 chs, sk next 2 chs, sc dec over next 2 chs; sc in next 4 chs, 2 sc in last ch, turn. *(27 sts and chs)*

Row 2: Ch 1, hdc in first st, **bsc** *(See Special Stitches)* in same st, bsc in next 4 sts, ch 1, sk next 3 sts, bsc in next 4 sts, (bsc, ch 1, bsc) in next ch-1 sp; bsc in next 4 sts, ch 1, sk next 3 sts, bsc in next 4 sts, (bsc, hdc) in last st, turn.

Row 3: Ch 1, (hdc, sc) in first st; sc in next 4 sts, **long sc** *(see Special Stitches)* in 2nd skipped st on row before last, sc in next 4 sts,

sc in next ch-1 sp, long sc in ch-1 sp on row before last, sc in same ch-1 sp on last row, sc in next 4 sts, long sc in 2nd skipped st on row before last, sc in next 4 sts, (sc, hdc) in last st, turn.

Row 4: Ch 1, (hdc, bsc) in first st; bsc in next 4 sts, ch 1, sk next 3 sts, bsc in next 4 sts, (hdc, ch 1, hdc) in next st; bsc in next 4 sts, ch 1, sk next 3 sts, bsc in next 4 sts, (bsc, hdc) in last st, turn.

Row 5: Ch 1, (hdc, sc) in first st; sc in next 4 sts, working over next ch-1 sp, long sc in center of long sc on row before last, sc in next 4 sts, sc in next ch-1 sp, long sc in center of long sc on row before last, sc in same ch-1 sp on last row, sk next hdc, sc in next 4 sts, long sc in center of long sc on row before last, sk next st, sc in next 4 sts, (sc, hdc) in last st, turn.

Rep Rows 4 and 5 for desired length, ending with Row 5. Fasten off.

Striped Zigzag Rug

Design by Donna Jones

Using a tweed yarn and a large crochet hook, it won't be long before you have a handsome throw rug with nice texture and versatility.

 **EASY**

Finished Size
Approximately 21 x 32 inches

Materials
Coats & Clark Red Heart Tweed medium (worsted) weight yarn:
    24 oz/1680 yds/680g
    #7071 Irish coffee
K/10½/6.5mm crochet hook or size hook needed to obtain gauge

Gauge
With **2 strands yarn** held tog:
2 sts = 1 inch; 2 rows = 1 inch

Rug
*Note: For **sc dec**, pull up lp in each of next 2 sts indicated, yo and draw through all 3 lps on hook.*

Row 1 (RS): With 2 strands yarn held tog, ch 74, 2 sc in 2nd ch from hook, sc in next 4 chs, sk next 2 chs, **sc dec** *(see Note)* over next 2 chs, sc in next 4 chs, *(sc, ch 1, sc) in next ch, sc in next 4 chs; sk next 2 chs, sc dec over next 2 chs; sc in next 4 chs; rep from * to last ch, 2 sc in last ch, turn. *(73 sts and chs)*

Row 2: Ch 1, hdc in first st, **bsc** *(See Special Stitches on page 66)* in same st; bsc in next 4 sts, ch 1, sk next 3 sts, bsc in next 4 sts, *(bsc, ch 1, bsc) in next ch-1 sp; bsc in next 4 sts, ch 1, sk next 3 sts, bsc in next 4 sts; rep from * to last st, (bsc, hdc) in last st, turn.

Row 3: Ch 1, (hdc, sc) in first st; sc in next 4 sts, **long sc** *(see Special Stitches on page 66)* in 2nd skipped st on row before last, sc in next 4 sts, *sc in next ch-1 sp, long sc in ch-1 sp on row before last, sc in same ch-1 sp on last row, sc in next 4 sts, long sc in 2nd skipped st on row before last, sc in next 4 sts; rep from * to last st, (sc, hdc) in last st, turn.

Row 4: Ch 1, (hdc, bsc) in first st; bsc in next 4 sts, ch 1, sk next 3 sts, bsc in next 4 sts, *(hdc, ch 1, hdc) in next st; bsc in next 4 sts, ch 1, sk next 3 sts, bsc in next 4 sts; rep from * to last st, (bsc, hdc) in last st, turn.

Continued on page 80

Rickrack Ripple

The stripes in this pattern are simply long single crochets worked into the previous rows. Subtle zigzags are evident in this ripple style design.

Knit

Crochet

Crochet Stitch Pattern

Special Stitches

For **cluster (cl),** [yo, pull up lp in next st indicated, yo, pull through 2 lps on hook] 3 times, yo, pull through all 4 lps on hook.

For **single crochet cluster (sc cl),** [pull up lp in next st indicated] 3 times, yo, draw through all 4 lps on hook.

For **decrease (dec),** [yo, pull up lp in next st indicated, yo, draw through 2 lps on hook] 2 times, yo, draw through all 3 lps on hook.

Multiple 6 sts + 11

*Note: When **changing colors**, drop last color, pick up again when needed. Do not cut unless otherwise stated.*

Row 1: With A, ch 17, dc in 4th ch from hook, dc in next ch, **cl** *(see Special Stitches)* over next 3 chs, dc in next st, 3 dc in next ch, dc in next ch, cl over next 3 chs, dc in next 3 chs, turn. *(13 sts)*

Row 2: Ch 3 *(counts as first dc)*, dc in same st, dc in next st, cl over next 3 sts, dc in next st, 3 dc in next st, dc in next st, cl over next 3 sts, dc in next st, 2 dc in next st changing to B in last st, turn.

Rows 3 & 4: Ch 1, 2 sc in first st, sc in next st, **sc cl** *(see Special Stitches)* over next 3 sts, sc in next st, 3 sc in next st, sc in next st, sc cl over next 2 sts, sc in next st, 2 sc in last st changing to A in last st, turn.

Rows 5 & 6: (Ch 3, dc) in first st, dc in next

st, cl over next 3 sts, dc in next st, 3 dc in next st, dc in next st, cl over next 3 sts, dc in next st, 2 dc in last st, turn.

Rep Rows 3–6 for pattern.

Rickrack Ripple Pot Holder
Design by Donna Jones

Using cotton yarn, fashion this handy, colorful pot holder in colors that complement your kitchen decor. Make a few extra, and you'll have appreciated hostess gifts always on hand.

 EASY

Finished Size
Approximately 7 x 7½ inches

Materials
Lion Brand Kitchen Cotton medium (worsted) weight cotton yarn:
  3 oz #186 maize (A)
  3 oz #181 sage (B)
Size K/10½/6.5mm crochet hook or size hook needed to obtain gauge

Gauge
7 sts = 2 inches; 2 dc rows = 2 inches

Pot Holder
Row 1: With B, ch 26, dc in 2nd ch from hook and in next ch, 3 dc in next ch, dc in next ch, [**cl** *(see Special Stitches)* over next 3 chs, dc in next ch, 3 dc in next ch, dc in next ch] 3 times, dec over last 2 chs. *(25 sts)* Fasten off.

Row 2: Working on opposite side in unused lps of beg ch, join A with a sl st in first lp, ch 3 *(counts as first dc)*, dc in same lp, dc in next lp, cl over next 3 lps, dc in next lp [3 dc in next lp, dc in next lp, cl over next 3 lps, dc in next lp] 3 times, 2 dc in last ch, turn.

Row 3: (Ch 3, dc) in first st, dc in next st, cl over next 3 sts, dc in next st, [3 dc in next st, dc in next st, cl over next 3 sts, dc in next st] 3 times, 2 dc in lst st changing to B in last st, turn.

Rows 4 & 5: Ch 1, 2 sc in first st, sc in next st, **sc cl** *(see Special Stitches on page 69)* over next 3 sts, sc in next st, [3 sc in next st, sc in next st, sc cl over next 3 sts, sc in next st] 3 times, 2 sc in last st changing to A in last st, turn.

Rows 6 & 7: (Ch 3, dc) in first st, dc in next st, cl over next 3 sts, dc in next st, [3 dc in next st, dc in next st, cl over next 3 sts, dc in next st] 3 times, 2 dc in last st changing to B in last st, turn.

Rows 8–15: [Rep Rows 4–7] 2 times.

Row 16: With B, (ch 3, dc) in first st, dc in next st, cl over next 3 sts, dc in next st, [3 dc in next st, dc in next st, cl over next 3 sts, dc in next st] 3 times, 2 dc in last st. Do not fasten off.

Edging
Working in ends of rows along side and spacing sts evenly, ch 1, sc in ends of rows across. Fasten off.
Working in ends of rows on opposite side, join B with a sc in end of Row 1, ch 1, sc evenly in ends of rows across. Do not fasten off.

Hanger
Ch 12, join with sl st in same sc as ch-12 to form ring; **do not turn,** sl st in **back lp** only *(see Stitch Guide)* of each ch. Fasten off. ❧

Bobbles in a Square

Combining stitches in a new way, this pattern is composed with bobbles, regular, backward and long single crochets and slip stitches.

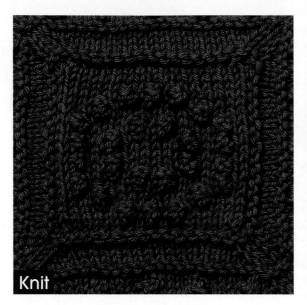

Knit

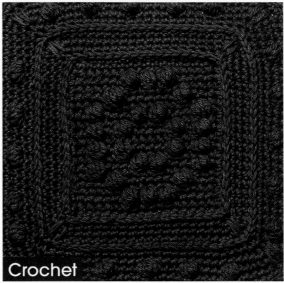

Crochet

Crochet Stitch Pattern

Special Stitches

To **hook yarn,** wrap yarn clockwise around hook. *Note: A regular yarn over (yo) is wrapped counterclockwise.*

For **backward single crochet (bsc),** with WS of work facing you and holding hook behind yarn, insert hook from back to front through next st, **hook yarn** *(see above),* pull through st, yo, draw through 2 lps on hook.

For **bobble,** [yo, pull up lp in st, yo, draw through 2 lps on hook] 4 times all in st indicated, yo, draw through all 5 lps on hook.

For **back post single crochet (bpsc),** insert hook from back to front around post *(see Stitch Guide)* of st indicated, pull up lp, yo, draw through 2 lps on hook.

For **long single crochet (long sc),** pull up lp in corresponding st on 2nd row below, pull up to height of row being worked, complete as sc.

Bobble Square

Multiple of 17 sts +1

Row 1 (RS): Ch 18, sc in 2nd ch from hook and in each ch across, turn. *(17 sc)*

Row 2 & all even-numbered rows: Ch 1, **bsc** *(see Special Stitches)* in each st across, turn.

Row 3: Ch 1, sc in first 6 sts, **bobble** *(see Special Stitches)* in next st, [sc in next st, bobble in next st] 2 times, sc in next 6 sts, turn.

Row 5: Ch 1, sc in first 4 sts, bobble, sc in next 7 sts, bobble, sc in next 4 sts, turn.
Row 7: Ch 1, sc in first 2 sts, bobble, sc in next 4 sts, bobble, sc in next st, bobble, sc in next 4 sts, bobble, sc in next 2 sts, turn.

Row 9: Ch 1, sc in first 2 sts, bobble, sc in next 2 sts, bobble, sc in next 5 sts, [bobble, sc in next 2 sts] 2 times, turn.

Row 11: Rep Row 9.

Row 13: Rep Row 7.

Row 15: Rep Row 5.

Row 17: Ch 1, sc in first 6 sts, bobble, [sc in next st, bobble] 2 times, sc in next 6 sts, turn.

Row 18: Ch 1, bsc in each st across. Fasten off.

Bobbles-in-a-Square Hot Pad

Design by Donna Jones

Suited to your entertaining and everyday dining needs, this hot pad features a fresh approach to bobbles. After crocheting the center bobble square, a bobbled border is added around all four sides.

 EASY

Finished Size
Approximately 8½ inches square

Materials
Lion Brand Lion Cotton medium (worsted) weight yarn:
5 oz/236 yds/140g #135 cinnamon
Size G/6/4mm hook or size hook needed to obtain gauge

4 MEDIUM

Gauge
8 sts = 2 inches; 9 rows = 2 inches

Hot Pad
Bobble Square Center
Work Rows 1–18 of Bobble Square pattern on page 72.

Row 19: Ch 1, sc in each st across, do not turn.

Border
Rnd 1: Ch 1; working in ends of rows, work 17 sc evenly spaced to next corner; working in unused lps of beg chs, sc in next 17 lps; working in ends of rows on next side, work 17 sc evenly spaced to next corner, working across Row 19, sc in each st across, join with sl st in first sc. *(17 sts on each side)*

Rnd 2: Ch 1, sk first sc, **bpsc** *(see Special Stitches on page 72)* around next 16 sts; [2 bpsc around next st *(corner made)*, bpsc around next 16 sts] 3 times, 2 bpsc around first st *(corner made)*, join. *(18 sts on each side)*

Rnd 3: Ch 1, [sc in first 16 sts, 2 sc in each of next 2 corner sts] 4 times, join. *(20 sts on each side)*

Rnd 4: Ch 1, sc in first 17 sts, 2 sc in each of next 2 sts, [sc in next 18 sts, 2 sc in each of next 2 sts] 3 times, sc in next st, join. *(22 sts on each side)*

Rnd 5: Ch 1, sc in first 19 sc, **long sc** *(see Special Stitches)* in top of corresponding st on 3rd rnd below, long sc in next sc on 3rd rnd below, *(do not sk sts behind long sc)*, [sc in next 22 sts on last rnd, long sc in top of each of corresponding st on 3rd rnd below, long sc in next sc on 3rd rnd below] 3 times, sc in next 3 sts, join. *(24 sts on each side)*

Rnd 6: Ch 1, bpsc around same st as joining and each rem st, join.

Rnd 7: Ch 1, sc in first 19 sts, 2 sc in each of next 2 sts, [sc in next 22 sts, 2 sc in each of next 2 sts] 3 times, sc in next 3 sts, join. *(26 sts on each side)*

Rnd 8: Ch 1, 2 sc in first st, sc in next 20 sts, 2 sc in each of next 2 sts, [sc in next 24 sts, 2 sc in each of next 2 sc] 3 times, sc in next 4 sts, join. *(28 sts on each side)*

Rnd 9: Ch 1, sc in first 2 sts, bobble, [sc in next 4 sts, bobble] 3 times, sc in next 3 sts, *2 sc in each of next 2 sts, sc in next 2 sc, bobble, [sc in next 4 sc, bobble] 4 times, sc in next 3 sts, 2 sc in each of next 2 sts, sc in next 2 sc, bobble, sc in next 2 sts, join. *(30 sts on each side)*

Rnd 10: Ch 1, sc in first 22 sts, long sc in corresponding st on 3rd rnd below, long sc in next st on 3rd rnd below, sk next 2 sts on last rnd, [sc in next 28 sts, long sc in corresponding sts of each of next 2 sts on 3rd rnd below, sk next 2 sts on last rnd] 3 times, sc in next 6 sts, join.

Rnd 11: Ch 1, sc in first 22 sts, 2 sc in each of 2 sts, [sc in next 28 sts, 2 sc in each of next 2 sts] 3 times, sc in next 6. *(32 sts on each side)*

Rnd 12: Sl st in each st around, join with sl st in first sl st. Fasten off. ✤

Long-Stitch Square Pillow
Continued from 62

Sew edges of first row tog. Sew edges of last row tog. Insert pillow form and sew ends of rows tog from corner to corner, as shown in Fig 2.

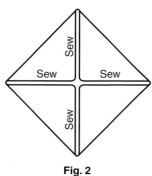

Fig. 2

Tassels (make 4)
For **tassel**, cut 2 (16-inch) strands yarn, fold 1 (16-inch) strand yarn in half; lay both aside. Wrap yarn 26 times around 5-inch cardboard square. Remove cardboard and run folded strand through lps; tie tightly. Tightly wrap other 16-inch strand 10 times around lps ½ inch below first knot, tie tightly. Weave ends back through tassel to hide. Cut lps, trim ends even.

Tie 1 tassel to each corner of pillow, run ends back through tassel to hide. ✤

Chain Links

Using a single crochet background the raised post stitches form a unique chain-link pattern.

Knit

Crochet

Crochet Stitch Pattern

Special Stitches

For **front post double crochet (fpdc),** yo, insert hook from front to back around post *(see Stitch Guide)* of st indicated, yo, draw lp through, [yo, draw through 2 lps on hook] 2 times. ***Note:*** *Sk st behind fpdc on last rnd.*

For **back post double crochet (bpdc),** yo, insert hook from back to front around post *(see Stitch Guide)* of st indicated, yo, draw lp through, [yo, draw through 2 lps on hook] 2 times. ***Note:*** *Sk st behind bpdc on last rnd.*

For **back post half double crochet (bphdc),** yo, insert hook from back to front around post *(see Stitch Guide)* of st indicated, yo, draw lp through, yo, draw through all 3 lps on hook.

For **back post single crochet (bpsc),** insert hook from back to front around post

(see Stitch Guide) of st indicated, yo, draw lp through, yo, draw through 2 lps on hook.

Multiple of 16 sts + 1

Row 1 (RS): Ch 17, sc in 2nd ch from hook and in each rem ch, turn. *(16 sc)*

Row 2 & all even-numbered rows: Ch 1, sc in each sc, turn.

Row 3: Ch 1, sc in first 3 st, **fpdc** *(see Special Stitches)* around 4th and 5th st on row before last, sk next 2 sts on last row, sc in next 6 sts, sk next 6 sts on row before last, fpdc around each of next 2 sts, sk next 2 sts on last row, sc in next 3 sts, turn.

Row 5: Ch 1, sc in first 3 sts, fpdc around each of next 2 fpdc, sk next 2 sts on last row, sc in next 6 sts, fpdc around each of next 2 fpdc, sk next 2 sts on last row, sc in next 3 sts, turn.

Row 7: Ch 1, sc in first 2 sts, fpdc around 3rd st on row before last, fpdc around each of next 2 fpdc, fpdc around next st, sk next 4 sts on last row, sc in next 4 sts, sk next 4 sts on row before last, fpdc around next st, fpdc around each of next 2 fpdc, fpdc around next sc, sk next 4 sts on last row, sc in last 2 sts, turn.

Row 9: Ch 1, sc in first sc, fpdc around 2nd st on row before last, fpdc around next fpdc, sk next 2 sts on last row, sc in next 2 sts, fpdc around next fpdc, fpdc around next st on row before last, sk next 2 sts on last row, sc in next 2 sts, sk next 2 sts on row before last, fpdc around next st, fpdc around next fpdc, sk next 2 sts on last row, sc in next 2 sts, fpdc around next fpdc, fpdc around next st on row before last, sk next 2 sts on last row, sc in last st, turn.

Row 11: Ch 1, sc in first st, fpdc around each of next 2 fpdc, sk next 2 sts on last row, sc in next 2 sts, fpdc around each of next 2 fpdc, sk next 2 sts on last row, sc in next

2 sts, fpdc around each of next 2 fpdc, sk next 2 sts on last row, sc in next 2 sts, fpdc around each of next 2 fpdc, sk next 2 sts on last row, sc in last st, turn.

Row 13: Ch 1, sc in first 2 sts, sk next fpdc, fpdc around next fpdc, around each of next 2 sts on row before last and around next fpdc, sk next 4 sts on last row, sc in next 4 sts, sk next fpdc, fpdc around next fpdc, around each of next 2 sts on row before last and around next fpdc, sk next 4 sts on last row, sc in next 2 sts, turn.

Row 15: Ch 1, sc in first 3 sts, sk next fpdc, fpdc around each of next 2 fpdc, sk next 2 sts on last row, sc in next 6 sts, sk next fpdc, fpdc around each of next 2 fpdc, sk next 2 sts on last row, sc in next 3 sts, turn.

Row 16: Ch 1, sc in each st, turn.

Rep Rows 7–16 for pattern.

Next row: Ch 1, sc in first 3 sts, fpdc around each of next 2 fpdc, sk next 2 sts on last row, sc in next 6 sts, fpdc around each of next 2 fpdc, sk next 2 sts on last row, sc in next 3 sts, turn.

Last row: Ch 1, sc in each st. Fasten off.

Chain-Links Tissue Cover

The perfect complement to bedroom, bath or living areas, this tissue box cover is quick to make and a joy to use.

 **EASY**

Finished Size
Fits standard 4½ x 4½ x 5-inch boutique tissue box

Materials
Coats & Clark Red Heart Classic medium (worsted) weight yarn:

3 oz/21 yds/85g
#827 light periwinkle
Size G/6/4mm crochet hook or size hook needed to obtain gauge

Gauge
8 sc = 2 inches; 8 sc rows = 2 inches

Note: *Pattern is worked in joined rows.*

Row 1: Ch 64, sl st in first ch to form ring, ch 1, sc in each ch around, join with sl st in first sc, turn. *(64 sc)*

Row 2 & all even-numbered rows: Ch 1, sc in each st around, join, turn.

Row 3: Ch 1, sc in first 3 sts, **fpdc** *(see Special Stitches on page 76)* around 4th and 5th st on row before last, sk next 2 sts on last row, [sc in next 6 sts, sk next 6 sts on row before last, fpdc around each of next 2 sts, sk next 2 sts on last row] 7 times, sc in next 3 sts, join, turn.

Row 5: Ch 1, sc in first 3 sts, fpdc around each of next 2 fpdc, sk next 2 sts on last row, [sc in next 6 sts, fpdc around each of next 2 fpdc, sk next 2 sts on last row] 7 times, sc in next 3 sts, join, turn.

Row 7: Ch 1, sc in first 2 sts, fpdc around 3rd st on row before last, fpdc around each of next 2 fpdc, fpdc around next sc, sk next 4 sts on last row, [sc in next 4 sts, sk next 4 sts on row before last, fpdc around next sc, fpdc around each of next 2 fpdc, fpdc around next sc, sk next 4 sts on last row] 7 times, sc in last 2 sts, turn.

Row 9: Ch 1, sc in first sc, fpdc around 2nd st on row before last, fpdc around next fpdc, sk next 2 sts on last row, sc in next 2 sts, fpdc around next fpdc, fpdc around next st on row before last, sk next 2 sts on last row, [sc in next 2 sts, sk next 2 sts on row before last, fpdc around next st, fpdc around next fpdc, sk next 2 sts on last row, sc in next 2 sts, fpdc around next fpdc, fpdc around next st on row before last, sk next 2 sts on last row] 7 times, sc in next st, join, turn.

Row 11: Ch 1, sc in first st, fpdc around each of next 2 fpdc, sk next 2 sts on last row, sc in next 2 sts, fpdc around each of next 2 fpdc, sk next 2 sts on last row, [sc in next 2 sts, fpdc around each of next 2 fpdc, sk

next 2 sts on last row, sc in next 2 sts, fpdc around each of next 2 fpdc, sk next 2 sts on last row] 7 times, sc in next st, join, turn.

Row 13: Ch 1, sc in first 2 sts, sk next fpdc, fpdc around next fpdc, around each of next 2 sts on row before last and around next fpdc, sk next 4 sts on last row, [sc in next 4 sts, sk next fpdc, fpdc around next fpdc, around each of next 2 sts on row before last and around next fpdc, sk next 4 sts on last row] 7 times, sc in next 2 sts, join, turn.

Row 15: Ch 1, sc in first 3 sts, sk next fpdc, fpdc around each of next 2 fpdc, sk next 2 sts on last row, [sc in next 6 sts, sk next fpdc, fpdc around each of next 2 fpdc, sk next 2 sts on last row] 7 times, sc in next 3 sts, join, turn.

Row 16: Ch 1, sc in each st, turn.

Rows 17–26: Rep Rows 7–16.

Note: *For **bpdc dec**, [yo, insert hook from back to front around post (see Stitch Guide) of next st, yo, draw lp through, yo, draw through 2 lps on hook] 2 times, yo, draw through all 3 lps on hook.*

Row 27: Ch 2, **bphdc** *(see Special Stitches on page 76)* around each of next 2 sts, fpdc around next 2 sts, **bpsc** *(see Special Stitches)* around next 6 sts, fpdc around each of next 2 sts, [bphdc around each of next 2 sts, **bpdc dec** *(see Note)*, bphdc around each of next 2 sts, fpdc around each of next 2 sts, bpsc around next 6 sts, fpdc around each of next 2 sts] 3 times, bphdc around each of next 2 sts, sk next st, join with sl st in top of ch-2, turn. *(60 sts)*

Note: *For **sc dec**, pull up lp in each of next 2 sts, yo and draw through all 3 lps on hook.*

Row 28: Ch 1, sc in same st and in next sts, **sc dec** *(see Note)*, sc in next 6 sts, sc dec, [sc in next 5 sts, sc dec, sc in next 6 sts, sc dec]

3 times, sc in next 2 sts, join in first sc, turn. *(52 sts)*

Row 29: Ch 1, hdc in first st, sc in next st, fpdc around next 2 fpdc, sk next 2 sts, sc dec, sc in next 3 sts, [fpdc around next 2 fpdc, sk next 2 sts, sc in next st, hdc in next 2 sts, sc in next st, fpdc around next 2 fpdc, sk next 2 sts, sc dec, sc in next 3 sts, fpdc around next 2 fpdc, sk next 2 sts] around to last 2 sts, sc in next st, hdc in last st, join in first hdc, turn. *(48 sts)*

Row 30: Ch 1, sc in first 2 sts, sc dec, [sc in next 4 sts, sc dec] around to last 2 sts, sc in last 2 sts, join, turn. *(40 sts)*

Row 31: Ch 1, sc in first st, fpdc around each of next 2 sts, [sc in next 3 sts, fpdc around each of next 2 sts] around to last 2 sts, sc in last 2 sts, join, turn.

Note: *For **3-sc dec,** pull up lp in each of next 3 sts, yo and draw through all 4 lps on hook.*

Row 32: Ch 1, sc in first st, sc next 3 sts tog, [sc in next 2 sts, **3-sc dec** *(see Note)*] around to last st, sc in last st, join, turn. *(24 sts)*

Row 33: Ch 1, sc in first st, fpdc around each of next 2 sts, sk next 2 sts, [sc in next st, fpdc around each of next 2 sts, sk next 2 sts] around, join, **do not turn.**

Row 34: Sl st in each st around, join in first sl st. Fasten off. ✤

Striped Zigzag Rug
Continued from 68

Row 5: Ch 1, (hdc, sc) in first st; sc in next 4 sts, working over next ch-1 sp, long sc in center of long sc on row before last, sc in next 4 sts, *sc in next ch-1 sp, long sc in center of long sc on row before last, sc in same ch-1 sp on last row, sk next hdc, sc in next 4 sts, long sc in center of long sc on row before last, sk next st, sc in next 4 sts; rep from * across to last st, (sc, hdc) in last st, turn.

Rep Rows 4 and 5 until piece measures approximately 32 inches, ending with a Row 5. Fasten off.

Fringe
For **fringe,** cut 7-inch strands of yarn. For each knot hold 3 strands of yarn tog as 1 and fold in half; insert crochet hook from back to front through st, pull fold through st, pull ends through fold, pull snug. Trim ends even. ✤

Chapter 4
For Baby

Look here for sweet and colorful ideas to give baby a warm welcome. This lineup of projects is great for finding ideas for baby shower gifting.

Ridged Shell

This pretty stitch is simply half double crochets for the shells and single crochets made in back loops for the ridges.

Knit

Crochet

Crochet Stitch Pattern

Special Stitch
For **shell,** work 3 hdc in st indicated.

Multiple of 3 sts + 6

Row 1 (RS): Ch 12, sc in 2nd ch from hook and in each ch across, turn. *(11 sc)*

Row 2: Ch 2 *(counts as a hdc)* sk next st, [**shell** *(see Special Stitch)* in next st, sk next 2 sts] 2 times, shell in next st, sk next st, hdc in last st, turn.

Row 3: Ch 1, sc in **back lp** *(see Stitch Guide)* only of each st across, turn.

Row 4: Ch 2, sk next st, [shell in next st, sk next 2 sts] 2 times, shell in next st, sk next st, hdc in last st, turn.
Rep Rows 3 and 4 for pat.

Last row: Ch 1, sc in each st across.

Ridged Shell Shirt

Design by Darla Sims

*Designed with flaps at the shoulders, this picture-perfect
T-shirt is soft and eacy to pull over baby's head.*

EXPERIENCED

Finished Sizes
6 [12, 24] months
Pattern is written for smallest size with changes for larger sizes in brackets.

Finished Chest Measurements
20 [22, 24] inches

Materials
Bernat Cotton Tots medium (worsted) weight yarn:

4 MEDIUM

8 oz/226g #90420 pretty in pink (A)
4 oz/113g #90421 strawberry (B)
Size G/6/4.25mm crochet hook
Size H/8/5mm crochet hook or size needed to obtain gauge
Yarn needle

Gauge
With larger hook: 6 sts = 2 inches

Back
Row 1 (RS): With larger hook and A, ch 33 [36, 39], sc in 2nd ch from hook and in each ch across, turn. *(32, 35, 38 sc)*

Row 2: Ch 2 *(counts as a hdc)* sk next st, *****shell** *(see Special Stitch on page 82)* in next st, sk next 2 sts; rep from * to last 3 sts, shell in next st, sk next st, hdc in last st, turn. *(10, 11, 12 shells)*

Row 3: Ch 1, sc in **back lp** *(see Stitch Guide)* only of each st across, turn.

Row 4: Ch 2, sk next st, *shell in next st, sk next 2 sts; rep from * to last 3 sts, shell in next st, sk next st, hdc in last st, turn.

Rep Rows 3 and 4 until back measures 6 [7, 8] inches, ending with a Row 4.
Place markers at each end of last row to mark armholes.
Continue in pattern until armhole measures approximately 3½ [4, 4½] inches, ending with a Row 3.
Place markers at each end of last row to mark shoulder line.

Back Left Overlapping Flap
Notes: *For **sc dec**, pull up lp in each of 2 sts indicated, yo, and draw through 3 lps on hook.
For **3-sc dec**, pull up lp in each of 3 sts indicated, yo and draw through all 4 lps on hook.*

Row 1 (WS): Ch 2, sk next st, [shell in next st, sk next 2 sts] 2 [2, 3] times, shell in next st, sk next st, hdc in next st, turn.

Row 2: Ch 1, **sc dec** *(see Notes)* over first 2 sts, sc in back lps only across, turn.

Row 3: Ch 2, sk next st, [shell in next st, sk next 2 sts] 2 [2, 3] times, 2 hdc in next st, hdc in last st, turn.

Row 4: Ch 1, **3-sc dec,** *(see Notes)* sc in back lps only across, turn.

Row 5: Ch 2, sk next st, [shell in next st, sk next 2 sts] 1 [1, 2] times, shell in next st, sk next st, hdc in last st, turn.

Row 6: Ch 1, sk first st, 3-sc dec over next 3 sts, sc in back lps only across.

For 6 (12) month sizes only
Row 7: Ch 2, sk next st, shell in next st, sk next st, hdc in next st, turn.

Row 8: Ch 1, sc in back lps only of each st. Fasten off.

For 24 month size only
Row 7: Ch 2, sk next st, shell in next st, sk next 2 sts, shell in next st, sk next st, hdc in next st, turn.

Row 8: Ch 1, sk first st, 3-sc dec over next 3 sts, sc in back lps only of each st. Fasten off.

Back Right Overlapping Flap
Row 1 (WS): With WS facing sk center 10 [13, 10] sts, attach yarn with sl st in next st, ch 2, sk next st, [shell in next st, sk next 2 sts] 2 [2, 3] times, shell in next st, sk next st, hdc in next st, turn.

Row 2: Ch 1, sc in back lps only to last 2 sts, sc dec, turn.

Row 3: Ch 2, 2 hdc in next st, [sk next 2 sts, shell in next st] 2 [2, 3] times, sk next st, hdc in next st, turn.

Row 4: Ch 1, sc in back lps only to last 3 sts, 3-sc dec, turn.

Row 5: Ch 2, sk next st, [shell in next st, sk next 2 sts] 1 [1, 2] times, sk next st, hdc in next st, turn.

Row 6: Ch 1, sc in back lps only to last shell, 3-sc dec.

For 6 (12) month sizes only
Row 7: Ch 2, sk next st, shell in next st, sk next st, hdc in next st, turn.

Row 8: Ch 1, sc in back lps only of each st. Fasten off.

For 24 month size only
Row 7: Ch 2, sk next st, shell in next st, sk next 2 sts, shell in next st, sk next st, hdc in next st, turn.

Row 8: Ch 1, sc in back lps only to last 3 sts, 3-sc dec. Fasten off.

Front
Work same as back until armhole measures 1½ [2, 2] inches less than back, ending with a Row 3.

Front Right Under Flap
Row 1 (WS): Ch 2, sk next st, [shell in next st, sk next 2 sts] 3 [4, 4] times, hdc in next st, turn, leaving rem sts unworked.

Row 2: Ch 1, sc dec over first 2 sts, sc in back lps only across, turn.

Row 3: Ch 2, sk next st, [shell in next st, sk next 2 sts] 2 [3, 3] times, hdc in next st, hdc in next st, turn.

Row 4: Ch 1, 3-sc dec over first 3 sts, sc in back lps only across. Fasten off.

Front Left Under Flap
Row 1 (WS): With WS facing, sk next 8 sts, attach yarn in next st, ch 2, [sk next 2 sts, shell in next st] 3 [4, 4] times, sk next st, hdc in next st, turn.

Row 2: Ch 1, sc in back lps only to last 2 sts, sc dec, turn.

Row 3: Ch 2, 2 hdc in next st, [sk next 2 sts, shell in next st] 2 [3, 3] times, sk next st, hdc in next st, turn.

Row 4: Ch 1, sc in back lps only to last 3 sts, 3-sc dec. Fasten off.

Neck Edging
*Note: For **picot**, ch 3, sl st in 3rd ch from hook.*

Continued on page 89

Balloon Stitch

Rounded areas of single crochet background are neatly outlined top and bottom with single crochets and in between with long double crochet stitches.

Knit

Crochet

Crochet Stitch Pattern

Special Stitches

For **long double crochet (long dc),** yo, insert hook in st indicated, yo, pull up lp to height of row before last row, [yo, draw through 2 lps on hook] 2 times.

For **popcorn (pc),** 5 dc in st indicated, remove lp from hook, insert hook in first dc, draw dropped lp through.

Multiple of 16 sts + 5
Note: *Pattern St is worked with a main color (A) and background colors (B and C); any number of background colors may be used.*

Row 1 (RS): With A, ch 21, sc in 2nd ch from hook and in each ch across, turn. *(20 sc)*

Row 2: Ch 1, sc in first st, [ch 2, sk next 2 sts, sc in next 6 sts] 2 times; ch 2, sk next 2 sts, sc in last st, changing to B in last st, turn.

Row 3: Ch 1, sc in first st, [2 sc in next ch-2 sp, sc in next 6 sts] 2 times; 2 sc in next ch-2 sp, sc in last st, turn.

Rows 4–7: Ch 1, sc in each st, turn.

Row 8: Ch 1, sc in each st, changing to A in last st, turn.

Row 9: Ch 1, sc in first st, [folding piece forward, **long dc** *(see Special Stitches)* in each of next 2 skipped sts on 7th row below, sk next 2 sts on last row, sc in next 6 sts] 2 times; folding piece

forward, long dc in each of next 2 skipped sts on 7th row below, sk next 2 sts on last row, sc in last st, turn.

Row 10: Ch 1, sc in first 5 sts, ch 2, sk next 2 sts, sc in next 6 sts, ch 2, sk next 2 sts, sc in next 5 sts changing to C in last sc, turn.

Row 11: Ch 1, sc in first 5 sts, 2 sc in next ch-2 sp, sc in next 6 sts, 2 sc in next ch-2 sp, sc in next 5 sts, turn.

Rows 12–15: Ch 1, sc in each st, turn.

Row 16: Ch 1, sc in each st, changing to

A in last sc, turn.

Row 17: Ch 1, sc in first 5 sts, folding piece forward, long dc in each of next 2 skipped sts on 7th row below, sk next 2 sts on last row, sc in next 6 sts, long dc in each of next 2 skipped st on 7th row below, sk next 2 sts on last row, sc in next 5 sts, turn.
Rep Rows 2–17 for pattern alternating background colors in desired sequence.

Next 2 rows: Rep Rows 2 and 3.

Last row. Ch 1, sc in each st. Fasten off.

Balloon Stitch Baby Afghan

Design by Darla Sims

Bright, happy rows of balloons make this afghan a fitting gift to welcome the new baby.

 EASY

Finished Size
Approximately 30 x 36 inches

Materials
Bernat Satin medium (worsted) weight yarn:
14 oz/664 yds/400g #04005 snow (A)
10.5 oz/498 yds/300g #04423 flamingo (B)
7 oz/332 yds/200g #04732 maitai (C)
7 oz/332 yds/200g #04742 lagoon (D)
Size G/6/4mm
Size H/8/5mm or size needed to obtain gauge

4 MEDIUM

Gauge
With larger hook: 14 sc = 2 inches

Row 1 (RS): With A, ch 101, sc in 2nd ch from hook and in each ch across, turn. *(100 sc)*

Row 2: Ch 1, sc in first st, [ch 2, sk next 2 sts, sc in next 6 sts] 12 times; ch 2, sk next 2 sts, sc in last sc, changing to B in last st, turn.

Row 3: Ch 1, sc in first st, [2 sc in next ch-2 sp, sc in next 6 sc] 12 times; 2 sc in next ch-2 sp, sc in last st, turn.

Rows 4–7: Ch 1, sc in each st, turn.

Row 8: Ch 1, sc in each st, changing to A in last st, turn.

Row 9: Ch1, sc in first st, [folding piece forward, **long dc** *(see Special Stitches on page 86)* in each of next 2 skipped sts on 7th row below, sk next 2 sts on last row, sc in next 6 sts] 12 times; folding piece forward, long dc in each of next 2 skipped sts on 7th row below, sk next 2 sts on last row, sc in last st, turn.

Row 10: Ch 1, sc in first 5 sts, ch 2, sk next 2 sts, [sc in next 6 sts, ch 2, sk next 2 sts]

11 times, sc in next 5 sts changing to C in last sc, turn.

Row 11: Ch 1, sc in first 5 sts, 2 sc in next ch-2 sp, [sc in next 6 sts, 2 sc in next ch-2 sp] 11 times, sc in next 5 sts, turn.

Rows 12–15: Ch 1, sc in each st, turn.

Row 16: Ch 1, sc in each st, changing to A in last sc, turn.

Row 17: Ch 1, sc in first 5 sts, folding piece forward, long dc in each of next 2 skipped sts on 7th row below, sk next 2 sts on last row, [sc in next 6 sts, long dc in each of next 2 skipped st on 7th row below, sk next 2 sts on last row] 11 times, sc in next 5 sts, turn.
Rep Rows 2–17 for pattern alternating background colors in sequence of D, B, C until afghan measures approximately 36 inches, ending with B and a Row 3 or Row 11.

Ridged Shell Shirt
Continued from 85

Row 1: Hold Back with RS facing, with smaller hook and A, sc evenly across flaps and neck edge. Fasten off.

Row 2: Attach B in first sc of Row 1, ch 1, sc in same st as joining and in next 2 sts, *picot, (see Note on page 85) sc in next 3 sts; rep from * across.
Fasten off.
Rep for Front neck edging.
Sew side seams to armhole markers.

Lower Edging
Hold shirt with lower edge at top, attach B in one seam, ch 1, sc in same st as joining and in next 2 sts, *picot, sc in next 3 sps; rep from * around adjusting sts as necessary to end with picot; join with sl st in first sc. Matching shoulder seams, pin front and back

Last row. Ch 1, sc in each st. Fasten off.

Side Edging
Row 1 (RS): Hold afghan with RS facing, with smaller hook attach A in side of first row of 1 long edge, ch 1, sc in same sp and evenly along edge keeping edge flat, turn.

Row 2: Ch 1, sc in each sc. Fasten off.

Rep Rows 1 and 2 on opposite side of afghan.

Bobble Edging
Rnd 1: Attach A to any corner st, ch 1, sc in same st and in each sc around, working 3 sc in each corner, join with a sl st in first sc.

Rnd 2: Ch 1, sc in same st as joining, sc in next 3 sc, *ch 4, sk next 2 sts, **pc** (see Special Stitches on page 86) in next st, ch 4, sk next 2 sts, sc in next st; rep from * around adjusting as necessary at end of rnd, join. Fasten off. ❖

flaps in place. Work through both thickness for sleeves.

Sleeves
Rnd 1: With larger hook, attach A at 1 underarm, work 26 [28, 30] sc evenly spaced around armhole, join with sl st in first sc.

Rnd 2: Ch 1, sc in same st as joining, *sc in next 3 sc, sc dec, rep from * around; join in first sc.

Rnd 3: Ch 1, sc in each st around; join. Change to B by drawing lp through.

Rnd 4: Ch 1, sc in same st as joining and in next 2 sc, *picot, sc in next 3 sts; rep from * adjusting sts as necessary to end with picot; join. Fasten off. ❖

Flower Garden

Watch posies bloom on a single crochet background as you crochet this fascinating combination of front post double crochets, long loops and popcorns.

Knit

Crochet

Crochet Stitch Pattern

Special Stitches

For **front post double crochet (fpdc),** yo, insert hook from front to back around post *(see Stitch Guide)* of st indicated, yo, draw lp through, (yo, draw through 2 lps on hook) 2 times.

For **popcorn (pc),** 5 dc in st indicated, remove lp from hook, insert hook in first dc, draw dropped lp through.

Multiple of 10 sts +12

Row 1 (RS): Ch 22, sc in 2nd ch from hook and in each ch across, turn. *(21 sc)*

Row 2 and all even-numbered rows: Ch 1, sc in each st across, turn.

Row 3: Ch 1, sc in first 5 sts, **fpdc** *(see Special Stitches)* around 6th sc on row before last, sk next st on last row, sc in next 9 sts, sk next 9 sts on row before last, fpdc around next st, sk next st on last row, sc in next 5 sts, turn.

Row 5: Ch 1, sc in first 5 sts, fpdc around next fpdc, sk next st on last row, sc in next 9 sts, fpdc around next fpdc, sc in next 5 sts, turn.

Row 7: Ch 1, sc in first 2 sts, *holding yarn at back of work, insert hook in skipped st behind fpdc on 5th row below, yo pull up lp to height of working row, yo, draw through 2 lps on hook *(long lp made),* sk st under lp on last row, sc in next 2 sts, fpdc around next fpdc, sk next st on last row, sc in next 2 sts,

holding yarn at back of work, insert hook in same skipped st behind fpdc on 5th row below, yo pull up lp to height of working row, yo, draw through 2 lps on hook *(long lp made)*, on last row sk st under lp, sc in next 3 sts; rep from * once more, ending rep with sc in last 2 sts, turn.

Row 9: Ch 1, sc in first 5 sts **pc** *(see Special Stitches on page 90)* in center of fpdc on row before last, sc in next 9 sts; pc in center of fpdc on row before last, sc in next 5 sts, turn.

Row 11: Ch 1, sc in first 10 sts, fpdc around next sc on row before last, sk next st on last row, sc in next 10 sts, turn.

Row 13: Ch 1, sc in first 10 sts, fpdc around next fpdc, sk next st on last row, sc in next 10 sts, turn.

Row 15: Ch 1, sc in first 7 sc, holding yarn at back of work, insert hook in skipped st behind fpdc on 5th row below, yo pull up lp to height of working row, yo, draw through 2 lps on hook *(long lp made)*, sk st under lp on last row, sc in next 2 sts, fpdc around next fpdc, sk next st on last row, sc in next 2 sts, holding yarn at back of work, insert hook in same skipped st behind fpdc on 5th row below, yo pull up lp to height of working row, yo, draw through 2 lps on hook *(long lp made)*, sk st under lp on last row, sc in next 7 st, turn.

Row 17: Ch 1, sc in next 10 sts, pc in center of fpdc on row before last, sc in next 10 sts, turn.

Row 18: Ch 1, sc in each st across, turn.

Rep Rows 3–18 for pat.

Flower Garden
Baby Cardigan & Bonnet

Design by Darla Sims

The ruffled edges of this precious hat and sweater add the perfect feminine note to the posied Flower Garden pattern stitch.

 **EASY**

Finished Sizes
6 [12, 24] months
Pattern is written for smallest size with changes for larger sizes in brackets.

Finished Chest Measurements
22 [24, 26] inches

Materials
Red Heart TCL Baby fine (sport) weight yarn:
12 oz/340g #7719 pinkie
Size F/5/3.75mm crochet hook
Size G/6/4mm crochet hook or size needed to obtain gauge
Yarn needle

Pattern Notes
Sweater is oversized to allow for growth.
Body is worked in one piece to armhole.

Body
Row 1 (RS): With larger hook, ch 92 [100, 110], sc in 2nd ch from hook and in each ch across, turn. *(91, 99, 109 sc).*

Row 2 and all even-numbered rows: Ch 1, sc in each st across, turn.

Row 3: Ch 1, sc in first 5 [4, 4] sts, **fpdc**

(see Special Stitches on page 90) around 6th [5th, 5th] sc on row before last, sk next st on last row, [sc in next 9 sts, sk next 9 sts on row before last, fpdc around next st, sk next st on last row] 8 [9, 10] times, sc in next 5 [4, 4] sts, turn.

Row 5: Ch 1, sc in first 5 [4, 4] sts, fpdc around next fpdc, sk next st on last row, [sc in next 9 sts, fpdc around next fpdc] 8 [9, 10] times, sc in next 5 [4, 4] sts, turn.

Row 7: Ch 1, sc in first 2 [1, 1] sts, *holding yarn at back of work, insert hook in skipped st behind fpdc on 5th row below, yo pull up lp to height of working row, yo, draw through 2 lps on hook (long lp made), sk st under lp on last row, sc in next 2 sts, fpdc around next fpdc, sk next st on last row, sc in next 2 sts, holding yarn at back of work, insert hook in same skipped st behind fpdc on 5th row below, yo pull up lp to height of working row, yo, draw through 2 lps on hook (long lp made), on last row sk st under lp, sc in next 3 sts; rep from * across, ending last rep with sc in last 2 [1, 1] sts, turn.

Row 9: Ch 1, sc in first 5 [4, 4] sts, *pc (see Special Stitches on page 90)* in center of fpdc on row before last, [sc in next 9 sts; pc in center of fpdc on row before last] 8 [9, 10] times, sc in next 5 [4, 4] sts, turn.

Row 11: Ch 1, sc in first 10 [9, 9] sts, [fpdc around next sc on row before last, sk next st on last row, sc in next 9 sts] 8 [9, 10] times, sk next st on last row, sc in next 1 [0, 0] st, turn.

Row 13: Ch 1, sc in first 10 [9, 9] sts, [fpdc around next fpdc, sc in next 9 sts] 8 [9, 10] times, sc in next 1 [0, 0] st, turn.

Row 15: Ch 1, sc in first 7 [6, 6] sc, *holding yarn at back of work, insert hook in skipped st behind fpdc on 5th row below, yo pull up lp to height of working row, yo, draw through 2 lps on hook; sk st under lp on last row, sc in next 2 sts, fpdc around next

fpdc, sk next st on last row, sc in next 2 sts, holding yarn at back of work, insert hook in same skipped st behind fpdc on 5th row below, yo pull up lp to height of working row, yo, draw through 2 lps on hook; sk st under lp on last row, sc in next 3 sts; rep from * across; sc in next 4 [3, 3] sts, turn.

Row 17: Ch 1, sc in next 10 [9, 9] sts, [pc in center of fpdc on row before last, sc in next 9 sts] 8 [9, 10] times; sc in next 1 [0, 0] st, turn.

Row 18: Ch 1, sc in each st across, turn. Rep Rows 3–18 until Body measures approximately 7 [7½, 8] inches, ending on a RS row.

Right Front
Row 1 (WS): Work in established pattern across 23 [25, 27] sts, turn.

Row 2: Ch 1, work in pattern across, turn. Rep Row 2 until armhole measures 2 [2½, 3] inches, ending with a RS row.

Shape Neck
Note: *For sc dec, pull up lp in each of next 2 sts indicated, yo and draw through all 3 lps on hook.*

Row 1 (WS): Ch 1, work in pattern to last 6 [7, 8] sts, turn, leaving rem sts unworked. *(17, 18, 19 sts)*

Row 2 (RS): Ch 1, **sc dec** *(see Note)* over first 2 sts, work in pattern across, turn. *(16, 17, 18 sts)*
Note: *If within 2 to 4 rows of completing Flower Pattern, work in sc only.*

Continue to work in pattern, dec 1 st, at neck edge, **every other row** 2 times more. *(14, 15, 16 sts)*

Next 2 rows: Ch 1, sc in each st across. Fasten off.

Left Front
Row 1 (WS): Hold piece with WS facing

and skipping next 45 [49, 55] sts, attach yarn in next st, ch 1, sc in same st, work in pattern to last 6 [7, 8] sts, turn, leaving rem sts unworked.

Row 2 (RS): Ch 1, work in pattern across.

Row 3: Ch 1, work to last 2 sts, sc dec, turn. Continue to work in pattern, work sc dec, at neck edge, **every other row** 2 times more. *(14, 15, 16 sts)*

Next 2 rows: Ch 1, sc in each sc, turn. Fasten off.

Back
Row 1 (WS): With WS facing, attach yarn with sc to first unused st to left of Right Front, sc in rem unused sts. *(45, 49, 53 sts)*

Work even in established pattern until armhole measures same as fronts. Fasten off.

Sleeves
Row 1 (RS): With larger hook, ch 24 [26, 28], sc in 2nd ch from hook and in each ch across, turn. *(23, 25, 27 sts)*

Row 2 and all even-numbered rows: Ch 1, sc in each st across, turn.

Row 3: Ch 1, sc in first 6 [7, 8] sts, fpdc around 7th [8th, 9th] sc on row before last, sk next st on last row, sc in next 9 sts, sk next 9 sts on row before last, fpdc around next st, sk next st on last row, sc in next 6 [7, 8] sts, turn. *Note: Place markers on each side of center 17 sts. Pattern is worked over these 17 sts from this point.*

Row 5: Ch 1, 2 sc in first sc (inc), sc in next 5 [6, 7] sts, fpdc around next fpdc, sk next st on last row, sc in next 9 sts, fpdc around next fpdc, sk next st on last row, sc in next 5 [6, 7] sts, 2 sc in last st (inc), turn. *(25, 27, 29 sts)*

Continue to work in pattern, inc 1 st each side, every 4th row 4 [5, 6] times more. *(33, 37, 41 sts)*

At the same time, when 4 [4, 5] Flower patterns are complete, work even in sc until sleeve measures 6 [7, 9] inches. Fasten off.

Finishing
Sew shoulder and sleeve seams. Matching seam of sleeve to underarm and center top of sleeve to shoulder seam, sew in sleeves.

Outer Edging
Rnd 1 (RS): Hold piece with RS facing, and beg ch at top, with smaller hook and beg below 1 armhole, attach yarn with sc, sc evenly spaced across lower edge, in ends of rows along front and along neck edge, working 3 sc in each corner to first shoulder seam, working across back, [sc in next 3 sc, sc dec] to next shoulder seam, sc evenly spaced along neck edge, in ends of rows along front and across lower edge, working 3 sc in each corner for first sc; join with sl st in first sc.

Rnd 2: Ch 3, 4 dc in same st as joining, 5 dc in each st around; join in 3rd ch of beg ch-3. Fasten off.

Sleeve Edging
Rnd 1 (RS): Hold sleeve with RS facing, with smaller hook attach yarn with a sc at sleeve seam, sc in each st around, join with sl st in first sc.

Rnd 2: Ch 3, 4 dc in same st as joining, 5 dc in each st around; join in 3rd ch of beg ch-3. Fasten off.

Rep for other sleeve.

Ties
With smaller hook, working under ruffle, attach yarn with sl st at front of neckline and make ch approximately 9 inches length for each side of neck. Fasten off.

Bonnet
Row 1 (RS): With larger hook, ch 46 [50,

54], sc in 2nd ch from hook and in each ch across, turn. *(45 49, 53 sc)*

Row 2 and all even-numbered rows: Ch 1, sc in each st across, turn.

Row 3: Ch 1, sc in first 5 sts, *fpdc around 6th sc on row before last, sk next st on last row, sc in next 9 sts, sk next 9 sts on row before last, fpdc around next st, sk next st on last row*, sc in next 13 [17, 21] sts, rep between ** once, in next 5 sts, turn.

Row 5: Ch 1, sc in first 5 sts, *fpdc around next fpdc, sk next st on last row, sc in next 9 sts, fpdc around next fpdc*, sk next st on last row, sc in next 13 [17, 21] sts, rep between ** once, sc in next 5 sts, turn.

Row 7: Ch 1, sc in first 2 sts, *holding yarn at back of work, insert hook in skipped st behind fpdc on 5th row below, yo, pull up lp to height of working row, yo, pull through 2 lps on hook *(long lp made)*, sk next st (under lp) on last row, sc in next 2 sts, fpdc around next fpdc, sk next st on last row, sc in next 2 sts, holding yarn at back of work, insert hook in same skipped st behind fpdc on 5th row below, yo pull up lp to height of working row, yo, pull through 2 lps on hook *(long lp made)*, sk next st on last row *(under lp)**, sc in next 3 sts; rep between ** once; sc in next 7 [11, 15] sts, rep between ** once, sc in next 3 sts, rep between ** once, sc in last 2 sts, turn.

Row 9: Ch 1, sc in first 5 sts, ***pc** in center of fpdc on row before last, sc in next 9 sts; pc in center of fpdc on row before last*, sc in next 13 [17, 21] sts, rep between ** once, sc in next 5 sc, turn.

Row 11: Ch 1, sc in first 10 sts, fpdc around next sc on row before last, sk next st on last row, sc in next 23 [27, 31] sts, fpdc around next sc on row before last, sk next st on last row, sc in next 10 sc, turn.

Row 13: Ch 1, sc in first 10 sts, fpdc around next fpdc, sk next st on last row, sc in next 23 [27, 31] sts, fpdc around next fpdc, sk next st on last row, sc in next 10 sts, turn.

Row 15: Ch 1, sc in first 7 sc, *holding yarn at back of work, insert hook in skipped st behind fpdc on 5th row below, yo pull up lp to height of working row, yo, pull through 2 lps on hook, sk next st *(under lp)* on last row, sc in next 2 sts, fpdc around next fpdc, sk next st on last row, sc in next 2 sts, holding yarn at back of work, insert hook in same skipped st behind fpdc on 5th row below, yo pull up lp to height of working row, yo, pull through 2 lps on hook, sk next st (under lp) on last row, sc in next 17 [21, 25] sts, rep between ** once, sc in next 7 sc, turn.

Row 17: Ch 1, sc in next 10 sts, pc in center of fpdc on row before last, sc in next 17 [21, 25] sts, pc in center of fpdc on row before last, sc in next 10 sts, turn.

Row 18: Ch 1, sc in each st across, turn. Rep Rows 3–18 once more

6 months size only, fasten off.

12 months size only, work 2 sc rows. Fasten off.

24 months size only, work Rows 3–18 once. Fasten off.

Finishing
Fold piece in half with WS tog and sew last row tog to form top of bonnet. Turn RS out.

Edging
Row 1: Hold bonnet with RS facing, with smaller hook and working in ends of rows, attach with an sc in edge of first row, sc evenly evenly around to opposite end of first row. Fasten off.

Continued on page 103

Cheerful Checks

This versatile pattern stitch employs double crochets that form the raised checks on top of a single crocheted background.

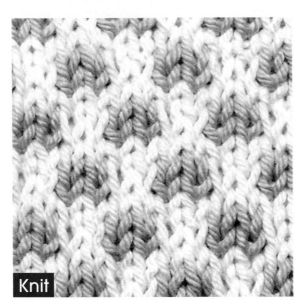

Knit

Crochet

Crochet Stitch Pattern

Multiple of 8 sts + 5

Pattern Note
Pattern stitch is worked in two colors; carry color not in use along the edge.

Row 1 (RS): With A, ch 13, sc in 2nd ch from hook and in each ch across, turn. *(12 sc)*

Row 2: Ch 1, sc in first st, [ch 2, sk next 2 sts, sc in next 2 sts] 2 times, ch 2, sk next 2 sts, sc in next st, changing to B in last sc, turn.

Row 3: Ch 1, sc in first st, [2 sc in next ch-2 sp, sc in next 2 sts] 2 times, 2 sc in next ch-2 sp, sc in next st, turn.

Row 4: Ch 1, sc in each st, across, changing to A in last sc, turn.

Row 5: Ch 1, sc in first st, [working in front of last 2 rows, dc in each of next 2 skipped sts on 3rd row below, sk next 2 sts on last row, sc in next 2 sts] 2 times, dc in each of next 2 skipped sts on 3rd row below, sk next 2 sts on last row, sc in next st, turn.

Row 6: Ch 1, sc in first 3 sts, [ch 2, sk next 2 sts, sc in next 2 sts] 2 times; sc in next st, changing to B, turn.

Row 7: Ch 1, sc in first 3 sts, [2 sc in next ch-2 sp, sc in next 2 sts] 2 times, sc in next sc, turn.

Row 8: Ch 1, sc in each st across, changing to A in last sc, turn.

Row 9: Ch 1, sc in first 3 sts, [working in front of last 2 rows, dc in each of next 2 skipped sts on 3rd row below, sk next 2 sts on last row, sc in next 2 sts] 2 times, sc in next st, turn.

Rep Rows 2–9 for pattern.

Cheerful Checks Baby Vest

Design by Darla Sims

Delightful to give, this fresh, checkered vest design is perfect for baby boys or baby girls.

Sizes
6 [12, 24] months
Pattern is written for smallest size with changes for larger sizes in brackets.

Finished Chest
20 [22, 24] inches

Materials
Lily Sugar Babies medium (worsted) weight yarn:
   5 oz/140g #01005 baby white (A)
   5 oz/140g #01215 baby aqua (B)
Size E/4/3.5mm crochet hook
Size G/6/4mm crochet hook or size needed to obtain gauge
Yarn needle

Gauge
With larger hook: 7 sts = 2 inches

Back
Ribbing
Row 1 (RS): With smaller hook and A ch 8, sc in 2nd ch from hook and in each ch across, turn. *(7 sc)*

Row 2: Ch 1, sc in **back lp** *(see Stitch Guide)* only of each sc, turn.

Rows 3–36 [40, 44]: Rep Row 2.

Body
Note: Do not cut yarn, carry yarn along edges throughout.

Row 1 (RS): Ch 1, working along side of ribbing in ends of rows, work 36 [38, 40] sc evenly spaced across, turn.
Change to larger hook.

Row 2: Ch 1, sc in first st, *ch 2, sk next 2 sts, sc in next 2 sts; rep from * to last 3 sts, ch 2, sk next 2 sts, sc in next st, changing to B in last st, turn.

Row 3: Ch 1, sc in first st, *2 sc in next ch-2 sp, sc in next 2 sts; rep from * to last 3 sts, 2 sc in next ch-2 sp, sc in next st, turn.

Row 4: Ch 1, sc in each st, across, changing to A in last st, turn.

Row 5: Ch 1, sc in first st, *working in front of last 2 rows, dc in each of next 2 skipped sts on 3rd row below, sk next 2 sts on last row, sc in next 2 sts; rep from * to last 3 sts, dc in each of next 2 skipped sts on 3rd row below, sk next 2 sts on last row, sc in next st, turn.

Row 6: Ch 1, sc in first 3 sts, *ch 2, sk next

2 sts, sc in next 2 sts; rep from * to last st; sc in last st, changing to B, turn.

Row 7: Ch 1, sc in first 3 sts, *2 sc in next ch-2 sp, sc in next 2 sts; rep from * to last st; sc in last st, turn.

Row 8: Ch 1, sc in each st across, changing to A in last st, turn.

Row 9: Ch1, sc in first 3 sts, *working in front of last 2 rows, dc in each of next 2 skipped sts on 3rd row below, sk next 2 sts on last row, sc in next 2 sts; rep from * to last st, sc in last st, turn.

Rep Rows 2–9 until Front measures 6½ [7, 8] inches, ending with a Row 5 or Row 9. Fasten off.

Armhole shaping
Row 1 (WS): Sk first 6 [6, 7] sts, attach yarn in next st, ch 1, sc in same st, work in established pattern to last 6 [6, 7] sts, turn, leaving rem sts unworked.

Row 2: Ch 1, work in pattern across, turn.

Work even in pattern until armhole measures approximately 4 [4½, 5] inches, ending with Row 5 or Row 9.

Last row: Ch 1, sc in each st across. Fasten off.

Front
Work Ribbing and Body as for Back to Armhole shaping.

Neck & armhole shaping
*Note: For **sc dec**, pull up lp in each of 2 sts indicated, yo, draw through all 3 lps on hook.*

Row 1 (WS): Sk first 6 [6, 7] sts, attach yarn in next st, ch 1, sc in same st, work in established pattern across next 9 [10, 10] sts, **sc dec** *(see Note)* over next 2 sts, turn, leaving rem sts unworked. *(11, 12, 12 sts)*

Row 2 (RS): Ch 1, work in pat across, turn.

Row 3: Ch 1, work in pattern to last 2 sts, sc dec, turn.

Row 4: Ch 1, work in pattern across, turn. Rep Rows 3 and 4 until 5 [6, 7] sts rem, turn.
Work even in pattern until armhole measures same as Back.

Last row: Ch 1, sc in each st across. Fasten off.

Second shoulder
Row 1 (WS): With WS facing, attach yarn in next st at neck edge, sc dec over next 2 sts, work in pattern to last 6 [6, 7] sts, turn, leaving rem sts unworked, turn. (11, 12, 12 sts)
Row 2 (RS): Ch 1, work in pattern across, turn.
Row 3: Sc dec over first 2 sts, work in pattern across, turn.
Row 4: Ch 1, work in pattern across, turn.

Rep Rows 3 and 4 until 5 [6, 7] sts rem, turn. Work even in pattern until armhole measures same as Back.
Last row: Ch 1, sc in each st across. Fasten off.

Finishing
Sew shoulder and side seams. With smaller hook and A, sc around armholes and neck edge. ✤

Horizontal Chevrons & Embossed Checks

Triple triple crochet are worked over single crochets to create this interesting chevron pattern. The raised checks are cleverly created with raised double crochets made in the front loops of previous single crochets.

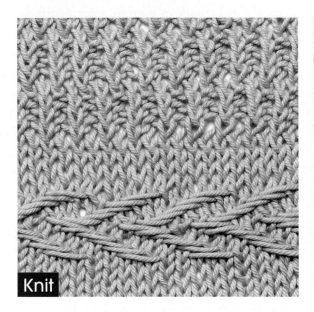

Knit

Crochet

Crochet Stitch Pattern

Special Stitches

For **front post triple treble crochet (fptrtr)**, yo 4 times, insert hook from front to back around post *(see Stitch Guide)* of st indicated, yo, draw lp through, [yo, draw through 2 lps on hook] 5 times.

For **front post double treble crochet (fpdtr)**, yo 3 times, insert hook from front to back around post *(see Stitch Guide)* of st indicated, yo, draw lp through, [yo, draw through 2 lps on hook] 4 times.

For **raised dc (rdc)**, yo, insert hook from top to bottom in lp of st indicated, yo, draw lp through, [yo, draw through 2 lps on hook] 2 times.

Horizontal Chevrons

Multiple of 6 sts + 9

Row 1 (WS): Ch 15, sc in 2nd ch from hook and in each ch across, turn. *(14 sts)*

Rows 2 & 3: Ch 1, sc in each st across, turn.

Row 4: Ch 1, sc in next 6 sc, **fptrtr** *(see Special Stitches)* around 2nd st of row before last, [sk next st on last row, sc in next 2 sts, sk next 2 sts on row before last, fptrtr around next st] 2 times; sk next st on last row, sc in next st, turn.

Row 5: Ch 1, sc in each st across.

Row 6: Ch 1, sc in next sc, **fpdtr** *(see Special Stitches on page 100)* around first post st, [sk next sc on last row, sc in next 2 sc, fpdtr around next post st] 2 times; sk next sc on last row, sc in next 6 sc, turn.

Row 7: Ch 1, sc in each st across, turn.

Rep Rows 2–7 for pattern.

Embossed Checks
Multiple of 6 sts + 3

Row 1 (WS): Ch 9, sc in 2nd ch from hook and in each ch across, turn. *(8 sc)*

Row 2 (RS): Ch 1, sc in each st, turn.

Row 3: Ch 1, sc in **front lp** *(see Stitch Guide)* only of each st across, turn.

Row 4: Ch 1, sc in first st, **rdc** *(see Special Stitches on page 100)* in 2nd lp on row before last, sk next st on last row, *sc in next st, sk next lp on row before last, rdc in next lp, sk next st on last row; rep from * across, turn.

Row 5: Ch 1, sc in front lp only of each st across, turn.

Row 6: Ch 1, sc in first 2 sts, rdc in 3rd lp on row before last, sk next st on last row, *sc in next st, sk next lp on row before last, rdc in next lp, sk next st on last row; rep from * to last st, sc in last st, turn.

Rep Rows 3–6 for pat.

Last row: Ch 1, sc in each st. Fasten off.

Horizontal Chevrons & Embossed Checks Baby Hat

Design by Darla Sims

We've featured two patterns on this one darling hat.
Who could resist a baby with curlicue tassels on her hat?

 **EASY**

Finished Size
6 [12, 24] months
Pattern is written for smallest size with changes for larger sizes in brackets.

Head Circumference
13¾ [14½,16] inches

Materials
Lily Sugar Babies medium (worsted) weight yarn:

5 oz/140g #01128 baby blue
Size F/5/3.75mm crochet hook
(for size 6 months)
Size G/6/4mm crochet hook
(for size 12 months)
Size H/8/5mm crochet hook
(for size 24 months)
Yarn needle

Gauge
With size F hook: 15 sts = 4 inches
With size G hook: 14 sts = 4 inches
With size H hook: 13 sts = 4 inches

Pattern Note
Hat size is determined by size hook used.

Front/Back (make 2)
Row 1 (WS): Ch 27, sc in 2nd ch from hook and in each ch across, turn. *(26 sts)*

Rows 2 & 3: Ch 1, sc in each st across, turn.

Row 4: Ch 1, sc in next 6 sts, **fptrtr** *(see Special Stitches on page 100)* around 2nd st of row before last, [sk next st on last row, sc in next 2 sts, sk next 2 sts on row before last, fptrtr around next st] 6 times; sk next st on last row, sc in next st, turn.

Row 5: Ch 1, sc in each st across.

Row 6: Ch 1, sc in next st, **fpdtr** *(see Special Stitches on page 100)* around first post st, [sk next sc on last row, sc in next 2 sts, fpdtr around next post st] 6 times; sk next st on last row, sc in next 6 sts, turn.

Rows 7 & 8: Ch 1, sc in each st across, turn.

Row 9: Ch 1, sc in **front lp** only *(see Stitch Guide)* of each st across, turn.

Row 10: Ch 1, sc in first st, **rdc** *(see Special Stitches on page 100)* in 2nd lp on row before last, sk next st on last row, *sc in next st, sk next lp on row before last rdc in next lp, sk next st on last row; rep from * across, turn.

Row 11: Ch 1, sc in front lp only of each st across, turn.

Row 12: Ch 1, sc in first 2 sts, rdc in 3rd lp on row before last, sk next st on last row, *sc in next st; sk next lp on row before last, rdc in next lp, sk next st on last row; rep from * to last st, sc in last st, turn.

Rep Rows 9–12 until piece measures approximately 6 [6¼, 6½] inches. Fasten off.

Curlicue Tassel (make 2)
Ch 15, 5 sc in 2nd ch from hook and in each of next 7 chs, sl st in next 6 chs. Fasten off.

Finishing
Pin Curlicue Tassel to outer corners at top of Front of hat. Pin Front and Back RS tog, sew side and top seams including end of Curlicue Tassel in seam. Turn RS out. ❧

Flower Garden
Baby Cardigan & Bonnet
Continued from 95

Row 2: Join in first sc, ch 3, 4 dc in same st as joining, 5 dc in each st. Fasten off.

Neck Edging
For **tie**, ch 40, sc in 2nd ch from hook and in each ch across. Fasten off and set aside.

Row 1 (RS): Hold bonnet with RS facing and lower edge at top, with smaller hook attach with an sc in first st, ch 1, sc in same st, *sc dec over next 2 sts, sc in next 2 sts; rep from * across, turn.

Rows 2 & 3: Ch 1, sc in each sc, turn.

Row 4: Ch 40, sc in 2nd ch from hook and in each ch across last row, pick up tie and sc in each ch. Fasten off. ❧

Daisy Stitch

Create this lovely pattern on a single crochet background by making three long loop stitches into the fourth row below.

Knit

Crochet

Crochet Stitch Pattern

Multiple of 8 sts + 10

Row 1 (RS): Ch 18, sc in 2nd ch from hook and in each ch across, turn. *(17 sc)*

Rows 2–6: Ch 1, sc in each sc across, turn.

Row 7: Ch 1, sc in first 2 sts, holding yarn at back of work, insert hook from front to back through 5th st 4 rows below, pull up lp to height of working row, [sk next st on last row (under lp), sc in next st, pull up lp in same st] 2 times *(daisy made)*, sk next st on last row (under lp), sc in next 3 sts, holding yarn at back of work, sk next 7 sts 4 rows below, insert hook from front to back through next st, pull up lp to height of working row, [sk

next st on last row (under lp), sc in next st, pull up lp in same st] 2 times *(Daisy made)*, sk next st on last row (under lp), sc in next 2 sts, turn.

Rows 8–14: Ch 1, sc in each st across, turn.

Row 15: Ch 1, sc in next 6 sts, sk first 8 sts on 4th row below, insert hook in next st, pull up lp, [sk next st on last row, sc in next st, pull up lp in same st] 2 times, sk next st, sc in next 6 sts, turn.

Rep Rows 2–15 for pattern.

Last 2 rows: Ch 1, sc in each st across. Fasten off.

Daisy Stitch Baby Afghan

Design by Darla Sims

Baby will enjoy the comforting warmth of this charming baby afghan featuring the distinctive daisy stitch pattern and cute floral border.

 **EASY**

Finished Size
Approximately 30 x 38 inches

Materials
Lion Brand Pound of Love medium (worsted) weight yarn:
    32 oz/2040 yds/908g #144 lavender
Size H/8/5mm crochet hook
Size I/9/5.5mm crochet hook or size needed to obtain gauge

Gauge
With larger hook: 6 sts = 2 inches

Afghan
Row 1 (RS): With larger hook, loosely ch 90, sc in 2nd ch from hook and in each ch across. *(89 sc)*

Rows 2–6: Ch 1, sc in each sc across, turn.

Row 7: Ch 1, sc in first 2 sts, holding yarn at back of work, insert hook from front to back through 5th st 4 rows below, pull up lp to height of working row, [sk next st on last row *(under lp)*, sc in next st, pull up lp in same st] 2 times *(daisy made)*, sk next st on last row *(under lp)*, *sc in next 3 sts, holding yarn at back of work, sk next 7 sts 4 rows below, insert hook from front to back through next st, pull up lp to height of working row, [sk next st on last row *(under lp)*, sc in next st, pull up lp in same st] 2 times *(daisy made)*, sk next st on last row *(under lp)*; rep from * 9 times more; sc in next 2 sts, turn. *(11 daisies)*

Rows 8–14: Ch 1, sc in each st across, turn.

Row 15: Ch 1, sc in next 6 sts, sk first 8 sts on 4th row below, insert hook in next st, pull up lp, [sk next st on last row, sc in next st, pull up lp in same st] 2 times, sk next st, *sc in next 6 sts, holding yarn at back of work, sk next 7 sts 4 rows below, insert hook from front to back through next st, pull up lp to height of working row, [sk next st on last row *(under lp)*, sc in next st, pull up lp in same st] 2 times; sk next st on last row *(under lp)*; rep from * 8 times more; sc in next 6 sc, turn. *(10 daisies)*

Rep Rows 2–15 until afghan measures approximately 36 inches, ending with Row 7 or Row 15.

Last 2 rows: Ch 1, sc in each st across. Fasten off.

Edging
Rnd 1: With RS facing and smaller hook, attach yarn with sl st in any st, ch 1, sc in same st, sc around, working 3 sc in each corner; join with sl st in first sc.

Rnd 2: *Ch 7, [sl st, ch 4] 5 times in 4th ch from hook *(flower made)*, ch 2, sk next 3 sts, sl st in next st; rep from * around adjusting number of skipped sts as necessary to have flower in each corner, and last sl st to join rnd. ❧

Chapter 5
For the Family

Create a layer of warmth and show your love with these appealing designs for man, woman and child. You'll enjoy the interesting textures and the way they look as stylish as a knitted garment.

Cherry Cluster & Zigzag

Create these clever clusters with popcorns, front post double crochets and back post single crochets on a sigle crochet background. Zigzags are formed vertically with front post double crochets and single crochets.

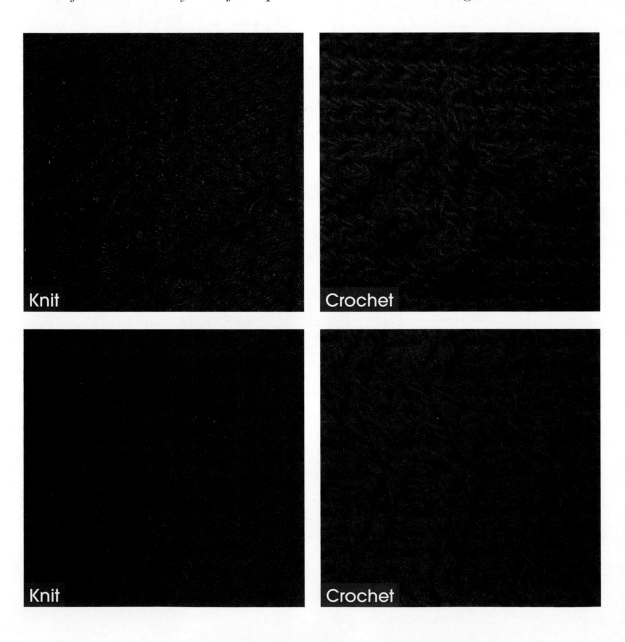

Knit

Crochet

Knit

Crochet

Crochet Stitch Pattern

Cherry Cluster
Special Stitches

For **popcorn (pc),** 4 sc in st indicated, remove lp from hook, insert hook in first sc, pull dropped lp through.

For **front post double crochet (fpdc),** yo, insert hook from front to back around post *(see Stitch Guide)* of st indicated, yo, draw lp through, [yo, draw through 2 lps on hook] 2 times.

For **back post single crochet (bpsc),** insert hook from back to front around post *(see Stitch Guide)* of st indicated, yo, draw lp through, yo, draw through 2 lps on hook.

For **front post double crochet decrease (fpdc dec),** [yo, insert hook from front to back around post *(see Stitch Guide)* of st indicated, yo, draw lp through, yo, draw through 2 lps on hook] 2 times, yo, draw through 3 lps on hook.

For **3-front post double crochet cluster (3-fpdc cl),** yo, insert hook from front to back around post *(see Stitch Guide)* of st indicated, yo, draw lp through, yo, draw through 2 lps on hook] 3 times, yo, draw through 4 lps on hook.

Multiple of 11 sts + 3

Row 1 (RS): Ch 14, sc in 2nd ch from hook and in each ch across, turn. *(13 sts)*

Row 2 & all even-numbered rows: Ch 1, sc in each st across, turn.

Row 3: Ch 1, sc in first 6 sts, **pc** *(see Special Stitches),* sc in next 6 sts, turn.

Row 5: Ch 1, sc in first 4 sts, *pc in next st, sc in next st, **fpdc** *(see Special Stitches)* around top of next pc on row before last, sk next st on last row, sc in next st, pc in next st, sc in next 4 sts, turn.

Row 7: Ch 1, sc in first 2 sc, pc in next st, sc in next st, fpdc around top of next pc, sk next st on last row, sc in next st, fpdc around next fpdc, sk next sc on last row, sc in next st, fpdc around top of next pc, sk next st on last row, sc in next st, pc in next st, sc in next 2 sts, turn.

Row 9: Ch 1, sc in first 5 sc, **fpdc dec** *(see Special Stitches)* around top of pc and next fpdc, fpdc around next fpdc, fpdc dec around next fpdc and top of next pc, sk next 3 sts on last row, sc in next 5 sc, turn.

Row 11: Ch 1, sc in first 6 sc, **3-fpdc cl,** *(see Special Stitches)* over next 3 fpdc, sk next st on last row, sc in next 6 sts, turn.

Row 12: Ch 1, sc in each st across.
Rep Rows 3–12 for pattern.

Zigzag
Special Stitch

For **front post double crochet (fpdc),** yo, insert hook from front to back around post *(see Stitch Guide)* of st indicated, yo, draw lp through, [yo, draw through 2 lps on hook] 2 times.

Multiple of 4 sts + 13

Row 1 (RS): Ch 17, sc in 2nd ch from hook and in each st across, turn. *(16 sc)*

Row 2 & all even-numbered rows: Ch 1, sc in each st across, turn.

Row 3: Ch 1, sc in first 6 sts, sk first 6 sts on row before last, fpdc around each of next 2 sts, sk next 2 sts on last row, sc in next 2 sts, sk next 2 sts on row before last, fpdc around each of next 2 sts, sk next 2 sts on last row, sc in next 4 sts, turn.

Row 5: Ch 1, sc in first 4 sts, fpdc around each of next 2 fpdc, sk next 2 sts on last row, sc in next 2 sts, fpdc around each of next 2 fpdc, sk next 2 sts on last row, sc in next 6 sts, turn.

Row 7: Ch 1, sc in first 2 sts, fpdc around each of next 2 fpdc, sk next 2 sts on last row, sc in next 2 sts, fpdc around each of next 2 fpdc, sk next 2 sts on last row, sc in next 8 sc, turn.

Row 9: Ch 1, sc in first 4 sts, fpdc around each of next 2 fpdc, sk next 2 sts on last row, sc in next 2 sts, fpdc around each of next 2 fpdc, sk next 2 sts on last row, sc in next 6 sc, turn.

Row 11: Ch 1, sc in first 6 sts, fpdc around each of next 2 fpdc, sk next 2 sts on last row, sc in

next 2 sts, fpdc around each of next 2 fpdc, sk next 2 sts on last row, sc in next 4 sc, turn.

Row 13: Ch 1, sc in first 8 sts, fpdc around each of next 2 fpdc, sk next 2 sts on last row, sc in next 2 sts, fpdc around each of next 2 fpdc, sk next 2 sts on last row, sc in next 2 sts, turn.

Row 15: Ch 1, sc in first 6 sts, fpdc around each of next 2 fpdc, sk next 2 sts on last row, sc in next 2 sts, fpdc around each of next 2 fpdc, sk next 2 sts on last row, sc in next 4 sts, turn.

Row 16: Ch 1, sc in each st across.
Rep Rows 5–16 for pattern.

Cherry Clusters & Zigzag Duster

Design by Darla Sims

For dressing up and doing the town, or dressing down, this duster is styled to handle it all.

 EASY

Finished Sizes
Small [medium, large, extra-large, 2X-large]
Pattern is written for smallest size with changes for larger sizes in brackets.

Finished Chest Measurements
40 [44, 48, 52, 56] inches

Materials
Brown Sheep Top of the Lamb medium (worsted) weight yarn:
190 yds/4 oz/113g per skein #420 red baron 12 [14, 16, 18, 20] skeins
Size J/10/6mm crochet hook or size needed to obtain gauge
Sizes K/10½/6.5mm and L/11/8mm crochet hooks
Yarn needle

Gauge
With J hook: 6 sts = 2 inches

Pattern Note
Duster is worked in one piece to armhole.

Duster
Border
Row 1 (RS): With largest hook, ch 124 [136, 148, 160, 172], sc in 2nd ch from hook and in each ch across, turn. *(123, 135, 147, 159, 171 sts)*

Row 2 & all even-numbered rows: Ch 1, sc in each st across, turn.

Row 3: Ch 1, sc in first 7 sts, ***pc** *(see Special Stitches on page 109)* in next st, sc in next 11 sts; rep from * 8 [9, 10, 11, 12] times more, pc in next st, sc in next 7 sc, turn.

Row 5: Ch 1, sc in first 5 sts, *pc in next st, sc in next st, **fpdc** *(see Special Stitches on page 109)* around top of next pc on row before last, sk next st on last row, sc in next st, pc in next st, sc in next 7 sts; rep from * 8 [9, 10, 11, 12] times more,

pc in next st, sc in next st, fpdc around top of next pc on row before last, sk next st on last row, sc in next st, pc in next st, sc in next 5 sts, turn.

Row 7: Ch 1, sc in first 3 sc, *pc in next st, sc in next st, fpdc around top of next pc, sk next st on last row, sc in next st, fpdc around next fpdc, sk next sc on last row, sc in next st, fpdc around top of next pc, sk next st on last row, sc in next st, pc in next st, sc in next 2 sts, rep from * 8 [9, 10, 11, 12] times more, pc in next st, sc in next st, fpdc around top of next pc, sk next st on last row, sc in next st, fpdc around next fpdc, sk next sc on last row, sc in next st, fpdc around top of next pc, sk next st on last row, sc in next st, pc in next st, sc in next 3 sts, turn.

Row 9: Ch 1, sc in first 6 sts, ***fpdc dec** (see Special Stitches on page 109)* around top of pc and next fpdc, fpdc around next fpdc, fpdc dec around next fpdc and top of next pc, sk next 3 sts on last row, sc in next 9 sc; rep from * 8 [9, 10, 11, 12] times more, fpdc dec around top of pc and next fpdc, fpdc around next fpdc, fpdc dec around next fpdc and top of next pc, sk next 3 sts on last row, sc in next 6 sts, turn.

Row 11: Ch 1, sc in first 7 sc, ***3-fpdc cl**, (see Special Stitches on page 109),* sk next st on last row, sc in next 11 sts; rep from * 8 [9, 10, 11, 12] times more, 3-fpdc cl, sk next st on last row, sc in next 7 sts, turn.

Row 13: Ch 1, **bpsc** *(see Special Stitches on page 109)* around each st across, turn.

Row 14: Ch 1, sc in each st across.

Body
Row 1 (RS): Ch 1, sc in first 6 sts, sk first 6 sts on row before last, *fpdc around each of next 2 sts, sk next 2 sts on last row, sc in next 2 sts, sk next 2 sts on row before last; rep from * to last 6 sts, fpdc around each of next 2 sts, sk next 2 sts on last row, sc in next 4 sts, turn.

Row 2 & all even-numbered rows: Ch 1, sc in each st across, turn.

Row 3: Ch 1, sc in first 4 sts, *fpdc around each of next 2 fpdc, sk next 2 sts on last row, sc in next 2 sts; rep from * to last 8 sts, fpdc around each of next 2 fpdc, sk next 2 sts on last row, sc in next 6 sts, turn.

Row 5: Ch 1, sc in first 2 sts, *fpdc around each of next 2 fpdc, sk next 2 sts on last row, sc in next 2 sts; rep from * to last 10 sts, fpdc around each of next 2 fpdc, sk next 2 sts on last row, sc in next 8 sc, turn.

Row 7: Ch 1, sc in first 4 sts, *fpdc around each of next 2 fpdc, sk next 2 sts on last row, sc in next 2 sts; rep from * to last 8 sts, fpdc around each of next 2 fpdc, sk next 2 sts on last row, sc in next 6 sc, turn.

Row 9: Ch 1, sc in first 6 sts, *fpdc around each of next 2 fpdc, sk next 2 sts on last row, sc in next 2 sts; rep from * to last 6 sts, fpdc around each of next 2 fpdc, sk next 2 sts on last row, sc in next 4 sc, turn.

Row 11: Ch 1, sc in first 8 sts, *fpdc around each of next 2 fpdc, sk next 2 sts on last row, sc in next 2 sts; rep from * to last 4 sts, fpdc around each of next 2 fpdc, sk next 2 sts on last row, sc in next 2 sts, turn.

Row 13: Ch 1, sc in first 6 sts, *fpdc around each of next 2 fpdc, sk next 2 sts on last row, sc in next 2 sts, fpdc around each of next 2 fpdc, sk next 2 sts on last row, sc in next 4 sts, turn.

Row 14: Ch 1, sc in each st across. Rep Rows 3–14 until piece measures approximately 10 inches.

Change to mid-size hook, work until piece measures 20 inches.

Change to small-size hook, continue to work in pattern until piece measures 33 inches or desired length to underarm, ending with a WS row.

Right Front

Row 1 (RS): Ch 1, bpsc in first 30 [33, 37, 40, 43] sts, turn.

Row 2: Ch 1, sc in each st across, turn.

Row 3: Ch 1, sc in first st, sc dec over next 2 sts, sc across, turn. *(29, 32, 36, 39, 42 sts)*

Row 4: Ch 1, sc in each st across, turn. [Rep Rows 3 and 4] 8 [8, 9, 9, 9] more times. *(21, 24, 27, 30, 33 sts)*

Yoke

Note: *For **sc dec**, pull up lp in each of 2 sts indicated, yo, draw through all 3 lps on hook.*

Row 1 (RS): Ch 1, sc in first sc, **sc dec** *(see Note)* over next 2 sts, sc in next 6 sc, pc, sc in each rem st, turn. *(20, 23, 26, 29, 32 sts)*

Row 2 & all even-numbered rows: Ch 1, sc in each st across, turn.

Row 3: Ch 1, sc in first sc, sc dec, sc in next 4 sts, pc in next st, sc in next st, fpdc around top of next pc on row before last, sk next st on last row, sc in next st, pc in next st, sc in each rem st, turn. *(19, 22, 25, 28, 31 sts)*

Row 5: Ch 1, sc in first 4 sc, pc in next st, sc in next st, fpdc around top of next pc, sk next st on last row, sc in next st, fpdc around next fpdc, sk next st on last row, sc in next st, fpdc around top of next pc, sk next st on last row, sc in next st, pc in next st, sc in each rem st, turn.

Row 7: Ch 1, sc in first 7 sc, fpdc dec around top of pc and next fpdc, fpdc around next fpdc, fpdc dec around next fpdc and top of next pc, sk next 3 sts on last row, sc in each rem st, turn.

Row 9: Ch 1, sc in first 8 sc, 3-fpdc cl over

next 3 fpdc, sk next st on last row, sc in each rem st, turn.

Row 10: Ch 1, sc in each st across, turn.

Rep Row 10 until armhole measures 9½ [10, 10½, 11, 11½].
Fasten off.

Back

Row 1 (RS): With RS facing and smallest hook, sk next st from right front, attach yarn with sl st in next st, bpsc around next 59 [65, 69, 75, 81] sts, turn.

Row 2: Ch 1, sc in each sc across, turn. *(59, 65, 69, 75, 81 sts)*

Rep Row 2 until armhole measures same as right front.
Fasten off.

Left Front

Row 1 (RS): With RS facing and smallest hook, sk next st from back, attach yarn with sl st in next st, bpsc in each st across, turn. *(30, 33, 37, 40, 43 sts)*

Row 2: Ch 1, sc in each st across, turn.

Row 3: Ch 1, sc in each st to last 3 sts, sc dec over next 2 sts, sc in last st, turn. *(29, 32, 36, 39, 42 sts)*

Row 4: Ch 1, sc in each st across, turn.

[Rep Rows 3 and 4] 8 [8, 9, 9, 9] more times. *(21, 24, 27, 30, 33 sts)*

Yoke

Row 1 (RS): Ch 1, sc in each st to last 10 sts, pc in next st, sc in next 6 sts, sc dec over next 2 sts, sc in next st, turn. *(20, 23, 26, 29, 32 sts)*

Row 2 & all even-numbered rows: Ch 1, sc in each st across, turn.

Row 3: Ch 1, sc in each st to last 12 sts, pc in next st, sc in next st, fpdc around top of next pc on row before last, sk next st on last row, sc in next st, pc in next st, sc in next 4 sts, sc dec over next 2 sts, sc in next st, turn. *(19, 22, 25, 28, 31 sts)*

Row 5: Ch 1, sc in each st to last 13 sts, pc in next st, sc in next st, fpdc around top of next pc, sk next st on last row, sc in next st, fpdc around next fpdc, sk next st on last row, sc in next st, fpdc around top of next pc, sk next st on last row, sc in next st, pc in next st, sc in next 4 sts, turn.

Row 7: Ch 1, sc in each st to last 10 sts, fpdc dec around top of pc and next fpdc, fpdc around next fpdc, fpdc dec around next fpdc and top of next pc, sk next 3 sts on last row, sc in next 7 sts, turn.

Row 9: Ch 1, sc in each st to last 9 sts, 3-fpdc cl over next 3 fpdc, sk next st on last row, sc in next 8 sts, turn.

Row 10: Ch 1, sc in each st across, turn.

Rep Row 10 until armhole measures same as back.
Fasten off.

Sleeve

Row 1 (RS): With smallest hook, ch 28 [28, 30, 30, 32], sc in 2nd ch from hook and in each ch across, turn. *(27, 27, 29, 29, 31 sts)*

Row 2 & all even-numbered rows: Ch 1, sc in each st across, turn.

Row 3: Ch 1, sc in first 13 [13, 14, 14, 15] sts, pc in next st, sc in rem 13 [13, 14, 14, 15] sts, turn.

Row 5: Ch 1, sc in first 11 [11, 12, 12, 13] sts, pc in next st, sc in next st, fpdc around top of next pc on row before last, sk next st on last row, sc in next st, pc in next st, sc in each rem st across, turn.

Row 7: Ch 1, sc in first 9 [9, 11, 11, 12] sts, pc in next st, sc in next st, fpdc around top of next pc, sk next st on last row, sc in next st, fpdc around next fpdc, sk next sc on last row, sc in next st, fpdc around top of next pc, sk next st on last row, sc in next st, pc in next st, sc in each rem st across, turn.

Row 9: Ch 1, sc in first 12 [12, 14, 14, 15] sts, fpdc dec around top of pc and next fpdc, fpdc around next fpdc, fpdc dec around next

Continued on page 139

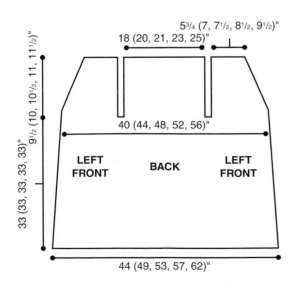

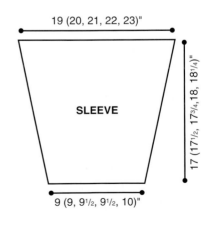

Raised Zigzag Pattern

As you work long single crochets over a regular single crochet background, this wonderful raised zigzag pattern will appear.

Knit

Crochet

Crochet Stitch Pattern

Special Stitch

For **long single crochet (long sc)**, insert hook from front to back in st indicated on 5th row below, draw lp through and up to height of working row, yo, draw through 2 lps on hook.

Multiple of 4 sts + 7

Note: *Pattern stitch is worked in 3 colors, one color (A) for the raised zigzag and two background colors (B, C), additional background colors can be used if desired.*

Row 1 (RS): With Color A, ch 19, sc in 2nd ch from hook and in each ch across, turn. *(18 sc)*

Row 2 & all even-numbered rows: Ch 1, sc in each sc across changing to B in last sc, turn.

Row 3: Ch 1, sc in each sc across, turn.

Row 5: Rep Row 3.

Row 6: Rep Row 2 changing to A in last sc, turn.

Row 7: Ch 1, *sc in next 3 sc, **long sc** *(see Special Stitch)* in 6th st on 5th row below, sk next sc *(under long sc)* on row below; rep from * to last 3 sts, long sc, sc in next 2 sc.

Row 8: Ch 1, sc in each sc across changing to C in last sc, turn.

Row 9: Ch 1, sc in each sc across, turn.

Row 11: Rep Row 9.

Row 12: Rep Row 2 changing to A in last sc, turn.

Row 13: Ch 1, sc in first 5 sc, *long sc in 4th sc on 5th row below, sc in next 3 sc; rep from * to last 2 sc, long sc, sc in last sc, turn.

Row 14: Ch 1, sc in each st across, turn.

Rep Rows 3–14 for pattern.

Raised Zigzag Top

Design by Darla Sims

This monochromatic color combination sets off the zigzag patterning and split neckline with aplomb.

 **EASY**

Finished Sizes
Small [medium, large, extra-large]
Pattern is written for smallest size with changes for larger sizes in brackets.

Finished Chest Measurements
38 [40, 42, 44] inches

Materials
Bernat Satin medium (worsted) weight yarn (163 yds/3.5 oz/100g per ball):
    3 [3, 4, 5] balls #04007 silk (A)
    2 [3, 4, 4] balls #04510 mango (B)
    2 [3, 4, 4] balls #04605 sunset (C)
Size F/5/3.75mm crochet hook
Sizes G/6/4mm or size needed to obtain gauge
Yarn needle

Gauge
With larger hook: 7 sts = 2 inches

Back
Row 1 (RS): With A and larger hook, ch 68 [72, 76, 80], sc in 2nd ch from hook and in each ch across, turn. *(67, 71, 75, 79 sc)*

Row 2 & all even-numbered rows: Ch 1, sc in each sc across changing to B in last sc, turn.

Row 3: Ch 1, sc in each sc across, turn.

Row 5: Rep Row 3.

Row 6: Rep Row 2 changing to A in last sc, turn.

Row 7: Ch 1, *sc in next 3 sc, **long sc** *(see Special Stitch on page 115)* in 6th st on 5th row below, sk next sc *(under long sc)* on row below; rep from * to last 3 sts, long sc, sc in next 2 sc.

Row 8: Ch 1, sc in each sc across changing to C in last sc, turn.

Row 9: Ch 1, sc in each sc across, turn.

Row 11: Rep Row 9.

Row 12: Rep Row 2 changing to A in last sc, turn.

Row 13: Ch 1, sc in first 5 sc, *long sc in 4th sc on 5th row below, sc in next 3 sc; rep from * to last 2 sc, long sc, sc in last sc, turn.

Row 14: Ch 1, sc in each st across, turn.
Rep Rows 3–14 until back measures 11 inches, ending with a WS row. Fasten off.

Shape armholes
*Note: For **sc dec**, pull up lp in each of next 2 sts, yo, draw through all 3 lps on hook.*

Row 1 (RS): With RS facing, sk first 8 [9, 10, 10] sts, attach yarn in next st, ch 1, sc in same

st, work in pattern as established to last 8 [9, 10, 10] sts, turn, leaving rem sts unworked.

Row 2: Ch 1, **sc dec** (*see Note on page 116*), work in pattern to last 2 sts, sc dec, turn.

Row 3: Ch 1, work in pattern across, turn.

Rep Rows 2 and 3 until back has 43 [45, 47, 51] sc.
Rep Row 3 until armhole measures 9 [9½, 10, 10½] inches.
Fasten off.

Front
Work as for back until armhole shaping is complete, ending with a RS row.

Neck shaping
First shoulder
Row 1 (WS): Work in pattern across first 20 [21, 22, 24] sts, turn, leaving rem sts unworked.

Row 2: Work in pattern across, turn. (*20, 21, 22, 24 sts*)
Rep Row 2 until armhole measures 6 [6½, 7, 7½], ending with a RS row.

Next row: Ch 1, work in pattern to last 5 [5, 5, 6] sts, turn leaving rem sts unworked. (*15, 16, 17, 18 sts*)

Next row: Ch 1, sc dec, work in pattern across, turn.

Next row: Ch 1, work in pattern across, turn.

{Rep last 2 rows} 5 times more. (*9, 10, 11, 12 sts*)
Work even in pattern until armhole measures same as back.
Fasten off.

Second shoulder
Row 1 (WS): Sk next 3 sts from first side, attach yarn in next st, ch 1, sc in same st, work in pattern across rem sts, turn.

Row 2: Work in pattern across, turn. (*20, 21, 22, 24 sts*)
Rep Row 2 until armhole measures 6 [6½, 7, 7½], ending with a WS row.

Next row: Ch 1, work in pattern to last 5 [5, 5, 6] sts, turn leaving rem sts unworked. (*15, 16, 17, 18 sts*)

Next row: Ch 1, sc dec, work in pattern across, turn.

Next row: Ch 1, work in pattern across, turn.

Continued on page 140

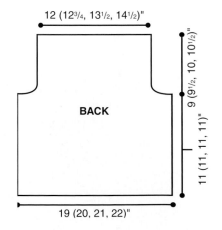

12 (12¾, 13½, 14½)"

BACK

9 (9½, 10, 10½)"

11 (11, 11, 11)"

19 (20, 21, 22)"

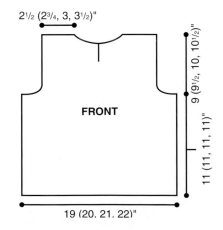

2½ (2¾, 3, 3½)"

FRONT

9 (9½, 10, 10½)"

11 (11, 11, 11)"

19 (20, 21, 22)"

Lattice Cables Stitch

*Classic cabling is the result of front post double crochets
with special right cross and left cross variations.*

Knit

Crochet

Crochet Stitch Pattern

Special Stitches

For **front post double crochet (fpdc),**
yo, insert hook from front to back around
post *(see Stitch Guide)* of st indicated, yo,
draw lp through, [yo, draw through 2 lps
on hook] 2 times. ***Note:*** *Sk st behind fpdc
on last row.*

For **right cross (RC),** sk next 2 fpdc, fpdc
(see above) around each of next 2 fpdc, fpdc
around each of 2 skipped fpdc.

For **left cross (LC),** sk next 2 fpdc, fpdc
(see above) around each of next 2 fpdc, fpdc
around each of 2 skipped fpdc.

Multiple of 26 sts + 3

Row 1 (RS): Ch 29, sc in 2nd ch from hook
and in each ch across, turn. *(28 sc)*

Row 2 & all even-numbered rows: Ch 1,
sc in each st across, turn.

Row 3: Ch 1, sc in first sc, **fpdc** *(see Special
Stitches)* around 2nd st on row before last, sk
next st on last row, sc in next 2 sts, fpdc on each
of next 2 sts on row before last, sk next 2 sts on
last row, sc in next 6 sts, sk next 2 sts on row
before last, fpdc around each of next 2 sts, fpdc
around each of 2 skipped sts, sk next 4 sts on last
row, sc in next 6 sts, fpdc around each of next 2
sts on row before last, sk next 2 sts on last row, sc
in next 2 sts, fpdc around next st on row before
last, sk next st on last row, sc in last st, turn.

Row 5: Ch 1, sc in first st, fpdc around next
fpdc, sc in next 3 sts, fpdc around each of
next 2 fpdc, sc in next 4 sts, fpdc around

each of next 2 fpdc, sc in next 2 sts, fpdc around each of next 2 fpdc, sc in next 4 sts, fpdc around each of next 2 fpdc, sc in next 3 sts, fpdc around next fpdc, sc in last sc, turn.

Row 7: Ch 1, sc in first sc, fpdc around next fpdc, sc in next 4 sts, fpdc around each of next 2 fpdc, sc in next 2 sts, fpdc around each of next 2 fpdc, sc in next 4 sts, fpdc around each of next 2 fpdc, sc in next 2 sts, fpdc around each of next 2 fpdc, sc in next 4 sts, fpdc around next fpdc, sc in last sc, turn.

Row 9: Ch 1, sc in first sc, fpdc around next fpdc, sc in next 5 sts, fpdc around each of next 4 fpdc, sc in next 6 sts, fpdc around each of next 4 fpdc, sc in next 5 sts, fpdc around next fpdc, sc in last sc, turn.

Row 11: Rep Row 9.

Row 13: Ch 1, sc in first sc, fpdc around next fpdc, sc in next 5 sts, **LC** (see Special Stitches on page 119), sc in next 6 sts, LC, sc in next 5 sts, fpdc around next fpdc, sc in last sc, turn.

Row 15: Rep Row 7.

Row 17: Rep Row 5.

Row 19: Ch 1, sc in first sc, fpdc around next fpdc, sc in next 2 sts, fpdc around each of next 2 fpdc, sc in next 6 sts, fpdc around each of next 4 fpdc, sc in next 6 sts, fpdc around each of next 2 fpdc, sc in next 2 sts, fpdc around next fpdc, sc in last st, turn.

Row 21: Rep Row 19.

Row 23: Ch 1, sc in first sc, fpdc next fpdc, sc in next 2 sts, fpdc on each of next 2 fpdc, sc in next 6 sts, **RC** (see Special Stitches on page 119), sc in next 6 sts, fpdc around each of next 2 fpdc, sc in next 2 sts, fpdc around next fpdc, sc in last st, turn.

Row 24: Ch 1, sc in each st across, turn.

Rep Rows 5–24 for pattern.

Lattice Cables Tunic

Design by Darla Sims

Timeless styling in sizes from small to 2X-large makes this tunic-style sweater an attractive choice for office or social occasions.

■■□□ EASY

Finished Sizes
Small [medium, large, extra-large, 2X-large]

Finished Chest Measurements
38 [40, 42, 44, 48] inches

Materials

Patons Katrina medium (worsted) weight yarn (163 yds/3½ oz/100g per ball):
  13 [15, 17, 18, 19] balls #10010 oyster
Size H/8/5mm crochet hook or size needed to obtain gauge
Yarn needle

Gauge
7 sts = 2 inches

Back
Row 1 (RS): Ch 71 [79, 85, 93, 99], sc in 2nd ch from hook and in each ch across, turn. *(70, 78, 84, 92, 98 sts)*

Row 2: Ch 1, sc in each sc across, turn. Rep Row 2 until back measures 18 inches.

Place markers at each end of last row to mark armholes. Continue to work Row 2 until Back measures 27 [27½, 28, 28½, 29] inches. Fasten off.

Front
Row 1 (RS): Ch 71 [79, 85, 93, 99], sc in 2nd ch from hook and in each rem ch across, turn. *(70, 78, 84, 92, 98 sc)*

Row 2 & all even-numbered rows: Ch 1, sc in each st across, turn.

Row 3: Ch 1, sc in first 21 (25, 28, 32, 25) sc, **fpdc** *(see Special Stitches on page 119)* around 2nd st on row before last, sk next st on last row, sc in next 2 sts, fpdc around each of next 2 sts on row before last, sk next 2 sts on last row, sc in next 6 sts, sk next 2 sts on row before last, fpdc around each of next 2 sts, fpdc around each of 2 skipped sts, sk next 4 sts on last row, sc in next 6 sts, fpdc around each of next 2 sts on row before last, sk next 2 sts on last row, sc in next 2 sts, fpdc around next st on row before last, sk next st on last row, sc in last 21 [25, 28, 32, 35] sts, turn.

Row 5: Ch1, sc in first 21 [25, 28, 32, 35] sts, fpdc around next fpdc, sc in next 3 sts, fpdc around each of next 2 fpdc, sc in next 4 sts, fpdc around each of next 2 fpdc, sc in next 2 sts, fpdc around each of next 2 fpdc, sc in next 4 sts, fpdc around each of next 2 fpdc, sc in next 3 sts, fpdc around next fpdc, sc in last 21 [25, 28, 32, 35] sts, turn.

Row 7: Ch 1, sc in first 21 [25, 28, 32, 35] sts, fpdc around next fpdc, sc in next 4 sts, fpdc around each of next 2 fpdc, sc in next 2 sts, fpdc around each of next 2 fpdc, sc in next 4 sts, fpdc around each of next 2 fpdc, sc in next 2 sts, fpdc around each of next 2 fpdc, sc in next 4 sts, fpdc around next fpdc, sc in last 21 [25, 28, 32, 35] sts, turn.

Row 9: Ch 1, sc in first 21 [25, 28, 32, 35] sts, fpdc around next fpdc, sc in next 5 sts, fpdc around each of next 4 fpdc, sc in next 6 sts, fpdc around each of next 4 fpdc, sc in next 5 sts, fpdc around next fpdc, sc in last 21 [25, 28, 32, 35] sts, turn.

Row 11: Rep Row 9.

Row 13: Ch 1, sc in first 21 [25, 28, 32, 35] sts, fpdc around next fpdc, sc in next 5 sts, **LC** *(see Special Stitches on page 119)*, sc in next 6 sts, LC, sc in next 5 sts, fpdc around next fpdc, sc in last 21 [25, 28, 32, 35] sts, turn.

Row 15: Rep Row 7.

Row 17: Rep Row 5.

Row 19: Ch 1, sc in first 21 [25, 28, 32, 35] sts, fpdc around next fpdc, sc in next 2 sts, fpdc around each of next 2 fpdc, sc in next 6 sts, fpdc around each of next 4 fpdc, sc in next 6 sts, fpdc around each of next 2 fpdc, sc in next 2 sts, fpdc around next fpdc, sc in last 21 [25, 28, 32, 35] sts, turn.

Row 21: Rep Row 19.

Row 23: Ch 1, sc in first 21 [25, 28, 32, 35] sts, fpdc next fpdc, sc in next 2 sts, fpdc on each of next 2 fpdc, sc in next 6 sts, **RC** *(see Special Stitches on page 119)*, sc in next 6 sts, fpdc around each of next 2 fpdc, sc in next 2 sts, fpdc around next fpdc, sc in last 21 [25, 28, 32, 35] sts, turn.

Row 24: Ch 1, sc in each st across, turn.

Rep Rows 5–24 for pattern placing markers for armholes as for back. Work in pattern until front is 6 rows less than back.

Shoulder shaping
First shoulder
Row 1: Ch 1, sc in next 21 [25, 28, 32, 35] sts, turn, leaving rem sts unworked.

Rows 2–6: Rep Row 1.
Fasten off.

Second shoulder
Row 1: Sk next 28 sts from first shoulder. Attach yarn in next st, ch 1, sc in same st and in rem sts across, turn. *(21, 25, 28, 32, 35 sts)*

Rows 2–6: Ch 1, sc in each st across, turn. Fasten off.

Sleeves
Row 1 (RS): Ch 29 [31, 33, 35, 37], sc in 2nd ch from hook and in each ch across, turn. *(28, 30, 32, 34, 36 sc)*

Row 2: Ch 1, sc in each st across, turn.

For **size small** only, [rep Row 2, inc 1 st, each end every 4th row] 18 times. *(64 sts)*

Continued on page 140

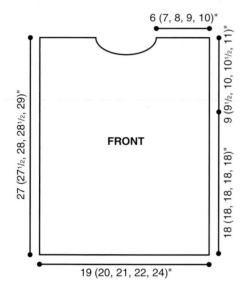

6 (7, 8, 9, 10)"

FRONT

27 (27½, 28, 28½, 29)"

9 (9½, 10, 10½, 11)"

18 (18, 18, 18, 18)"

19 (20, 21, 22, 24)"

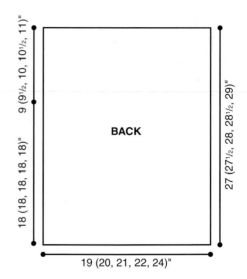

BACK

9 (9½, 10, 10½, 11)"

18 (18, 18, 18, 18)"

27 (27½, 28, 28½, 29)"

19 (20, 21, 22, 24)"

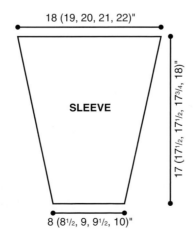

18 (19, 20, 21, 22)"

SLEEVE

17 (17½, 17½, 17¾, 18)"

8 (8½, 9, 9½, 10)"

Knotted Cables Stitch

This traditional cabled effect is fashioned with popcorns and front post double crochets.

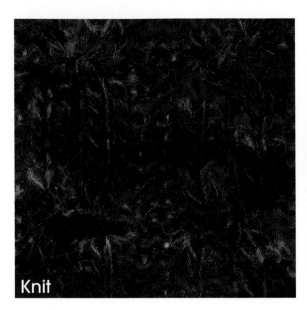

Knit

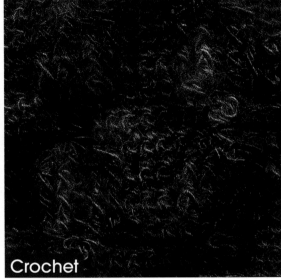

Crochet

Crochet Stitch Pattern

Special Stitches

For **front post double crochet (fpdc),** yo, insert hook from front to back around post *(see Stitch Guide)* of st indicated, yo, draw lp through, [yo, draw through 2 lps on hook] 2 times. Note: Sk st behind fpdc on last row.

For **front post double crochet decrease (fpdc dec),** [yo, insert hook around post *(see Stitch Guide)* of st indicated, yo, draw through, yo, draw through 2 lps on hook] 4 times, yo and draw through all 5 lps on hook.

For **popcorn (pc),** 3 dc around post *(see Stitch Guide)* of st indicated, remove lp from hook, insert hook in first dc, pull dropped lp through.

Multiple of 8 sts + 4

Row 1 (RS): Ch 12, sc in 2nd ch from hook and in each ch across, turn. *(11 sc)*

Row 2 & all even-numbered rows: Ch 1, sc in each sc across, turn.

Row 3: Ch 1, sc in first 3 sc, **fpdc** *(see Special Stitches)* around each of next 2 sts on row before last, sk next 2 sts on last row, sc in next sc, fpdc around each of next 2 sts on row before last, sk next 2 sts on last row, sc in last 3 sts, turn.

Row 5: Ch 1, sc in first 3 sc, fpdc around each of next 2 fpdc, sc in next sc, fpdc around each of next 2 fpdc, sc in last 3 sc, turn.

Row 7: Ch 1, sc in first 5 sc, **fpdc dec** *(see Special Stitches on page 124)* over next 4 fpdc, sk next sc on last row, sc in last 5 sc, turn.

Row 9: Ch 1, sc in next 5 sc, **pc** *(see Special Stitches on page 124)* around post of fpdc dec, sk next st on last row, sc in last 5 sc, turn.

Row 11: Ch 1, sc in first 3 sc, work 2 fpdc around 5th st on row before last *(st to right of pc)*, sk next 2 sts on last row, sc in next sc, work 2 fpdc around st to left of pc on row

before last, sk next 2 sts on last row, sc in last 3 sc, turn.

Row 13: Ch 1, sc in first 3 sc, fpdc around each of next 2 fpdc, sk next 2 sts on last row, sc in next sc, fpdc around each of next 2 fpdc, sk next 2 sts on last row, sc in last 3 sts, turn.

Row 14: Ch 1, sc in each sc across, turn.

Rep Rows 5–14 for pattern.

Knotted Cables Vest

Design by Darla Sims

The extraordinary cabled texture of this V-neck style vest is enhanced with the beautifully hued yarn.

 **EASY**

Sizes
Small [medium, large, extra-large, 2X-large]
Pattern is written for smallest size with changes for larger sizes in brackets.

Finished Chest Measurements
40 [44, 48, 52, 56] inches

Materials
Brown Sheep Handpainted Originals medium (worsted) weight yarn (88 yds/1¾ oz/50g per ball):
   12 [12, 13, 15, 17] balls
      #HP30 sunbaked earth
   Size G/6/4mm crochet hook
   Sizes I/9/5.5mm crochet hook or size needed to obtain gauge
   Yarn needle

Gauge
   6 sts = 2 inches

Back
Ribbing
Row 1: With smaller hook, ch 10, working in **back lps** *(see Stitch Guide)* only, sc in 2nd ch from hook and in each ch across, turn. *(9 sc)*

Row 2: Ch 1, working in back lps only, sc in each sc across, turn.
Rep Row 2 until 58 [66, 74, 78, 86] rows are complete.

Body
Row 1 (RS): Working along edge of ribbing in ends of rows, work sc 59 [67, 75, 79, 87] evenly spaced across, turn.

Row 2 & all even-numbered rows: Ch 1, sc in each sc across, turn.

Row 3: Ch 1, sc in first 3 [3, 3, 5, 5] sc, *__fpdc__ *(see Special Stitches)* around each of next 2 sts on row before last, sk next 2 sts on last row, sc in next sc, fpdc around each of next 2 sts on row before last, sk next 2 sts on last row, sc in next 3 sts; rep from * 6 [7, 8, 8, 9] times more, sc in last 0 [0, 0, 2, 2] sc, turn.

Row 5: Ch 1, sc in first 3 [3, 3, 5, 5] sc, *fpdc around each of next 2 fpdc, sc in next sc, fpdc around each of next 2 fpdc, sc in next 3 sc; rep from * 6 [7, 8, 8, 9] times more, sc in last 0 [0, 0, 2, 2] sc, turn.

Row 7: Ch 1, sc in first 5 [5, 5, 7, 7] sc, *fpdc dec *(see Special Stitches on page 124)* over next 4 fpdc, sk next sc on last row, sc in next 7 sc; rep from * 6 [7, 8, 8, 9] times more, ending last rep, sc in next 5 [5, 5, 7, 7] sc, turn.

Row 9: Ch 1, sc in next 5 [5, 5, 7, 7] sc, *pc *(see Special Stitches on page 124)* around post of fpdc dec, sk next st on last row, sc in next 7 sc; rep from * 6 [7, 8, 8, 9] times more, ending last rep, sc in next 5 [5, 5, 7, 7] sc, turn.

Row 11: Ch 1, sc in first 3 [3, 3, 5, 5] sc, *work 2 fpdc around 5th st on row before last *(st to right of pc),* sk next 2 sts on last row, sc in next sc, work 2 fpdc around st to left of pc on row before last, sk next 2 sts on last row, sc in next 3 sc; rep from * 6 [7, 8, 8, 9] times more, sc in last 0 [0, 0, 2, 2] sc, turn.

Row 13: Ch 1, sc in first 3 [3, 3, 5, 5] sc, *fpdc around each of next 2 fpdc, sk next 2 sts on last row, sc in next sc, fpdc around each of next 2 fpdc, sk next 2 sts on last row, sc in next 3 sts; rep from * 6 [7, 8, 8, 9] times more, sc in last 0 [0, 0, 2, 2] sc, turn.

Row 14: Ch 1, sc in each sc across, turn.

Rep Rows 5–14 until piece measures 16 inches, ending with a WS row.
Fasten off.

Armhole shaping
Note: For sc dec, pull up lp in each of next 2 sts, yo and draw through all 3 lps on hook.

Row 1 (RS): Sk first 4 [7, 9, 10, 13] sc, attach yarn with sl st in next st, ch 1, sc in same st, work in pattern to last 4 [7, 9, 10, 13] sts, turn, leaving rem sts unworked. *(51, 53, 57, 59, 61 sts).*

Row 2: Ch 1, **sc dec** *(see Note),* sc in each st to last 2 sts, sc dec, turn. *(49, 51, 55, 57, 59 sts)*

Row 3: Ch 1, work in pattern across.

Row 4: Ch 1, sc dec, sc in each st to last 2 sts, sc dec, turn.

Rows 5 & 6: Rep Rows 3 and 4. *(45, 47, 51, 53, 55 sts)*

Work even until armhole measures 9 [9½, 10, 10½, 11] inches, ending with a RS row.

Right shoulder shaping
Row 1 (RS): Ch 1, work in pattern across first 12 [13, 14, 14, 16] sts, turn.

Row 2: Ch 1, sc in each st across.
Fasten off.

Left shoulder shaping
Row 1 (RS): Sk next 21 [21, 23, 25, 23] sts from right shoulder, attach yarn with sl st in next st, ch 1, work in pattern across, turn. *(12, 13, 14, 14, 16 sts)*

Row 2: Ch 1, sc in each st across.
Fasten off.

Front
Work as for back to armhole shaping. Mark center st.
Sk first 4 [7, 9, 10, 13] sts, attach yarn with sl to next st, ch 1, sc in same st, work in pattern to last 4 [7, 9, 10, 13] sts, turn, leaving rem sts unworked. *(51, 53, 57, 59, 61 sts)*

Right neck & shoulder shaping
Row 1 (WS): Ch 1, sc dec, work in pattern

to 2 sts before center marker, sc dec, turn. *(23, 24, 26, 27, 28 sts)*

Row 2: Ch 1, work in pattern across, turn.

Rows 3–6: [Rep Rows 1 and 2] twice more. *(19, 20, 22, 23, 24 sts)*

Row 7: Ch 1, work in pattern to last 2 sts, sc dec, turn.

Row 8: Ch 1, work in pattern across, turn.

Rows 9 & 10: Rep Rows 7 and 8. *(17, 18, 20, 21, 22 sts)*
Dec 1 st at neck edge, every 4th row, 5 [5, 6, 7, 6] times. *(12, 13, 14, 14, 16 sts)*
Work even until armhole measures 9½ [10, 10½, 11, 11½], ending with a RS row.
Fasten off.

Left neck and shoulder shaping
Row 1 (WS): Hold front with WS facing, sk marked center st, attach yarn with sl st in next st, ch 1, sc in same st, sc dec, work in pattern to last 2 sts, sc dec, turn. *(23, 24, 26, 27, 28 sts)*

Row 2: Ch 1, work in pattern across, turn.

Row 3: Ch 1, sc dec, work in pattern to last 2 sts, sc dec, turn.

Row 4: Ch 1, work in pattern across, turn.

Rows 5 & 6: Rep Rows 3 and 4. *(19, 20, 22, 23, 24 sts)*

Row 7: Ch 1, sc dec, work in pattern across, turn.

Row 8: Ch 1, work in pattern across, turn.

Rows 9 & 10: Rep Rows 7 and 8. *(17, 18, 20, 21, 22 sts)*
Dec 1 st at neck edge, every 4th row, 5 [5, 6, 7, 6] times. *(12, 13, 14, 14, 16 sts)*
Work even until armhole measures 9½ [10, 10½, 11, 11½], ending with a RS row.
Fasten off.

Finishing
Sew shoulder and side seams.

Edgings
Armhole Edging
Rnd 1 (RS): With RS facing and smaller hook, attach yarn in 1 underarm seam, ch 1, sc in same st, sc around armhole, keeping edge flat, join with a sl st in first sc.

Rnd 2: Ch 1, sc in same st as joining and in each sc around; join.
Fasten off.
Rep for other armhole.

Continued on page 141

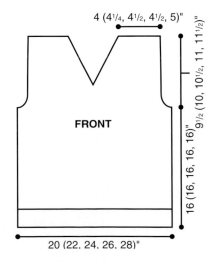

4 (4¼, 4½, 4½, 5)"

16 (16, 16, 16, 16)"

9½ (10, 10½, 11, 11½)"

BACK

20 (22, 24, 26, 28)"

4 (4¼, 4½, 4½, 5)"

16 (16, 16, 16, 16)"

9½ (10, 10½, 11, 11½)"

FRONT

20 (22, 24, 26, 28)"

Crisscross Stitch

Combine single crochets in a variegated yarn with long single crochets in a solid for this lighthearted pattern.

Knit

Crochet

Crochet Stitch Pattern

Special Stitch

For **long single crochet (long sc),** insert hook from front to back in st indicated, yo, pull up lp to height of last row, yo, draw through 2 lps on hook.

Multiple of 4 sts + 6

Note: *Pattern stitch is worked in 2 colors (A and B).*

Foundation row (WS): With A, ch 18, sc in 2nd ch from hook and in each rem ch changing to B in last sc, turn. *(17 sc)*

Row 1 (RS): Ch 1, sc in each sc across, turn.

Row 2: Ch 1, sc in each sc across changing to A in last sc, turn.

Row 3: Ch 1, sc in first 3 sc, **long sc** *(see Special Stitch)* in center of 6th st on 3rd row below, sk next st on last row, sc in next st, long sc in 2nd st to right of last long sc, sk next st on last row, sc in next st; *long sc in 4th st from last long sc, sk next st on last row, sc in next st, long sc in 2nd st to right of last long sc, sk next st on last row, sc in next st; rep from * once more, sc in last 2 sc, turn.

Row 4: Ch 1, sc in each st across changing to B in last sc, turn.

Row 5: Ch 1, sc in each sc across, turn.

Row 6: Ch 1, sc in each sc across changing to A in last sc, turn.

Row 7: Ch 1, sc in first sc, long sc in center of 4th st on 3rd row below, sk next st on last row, sc in next sc, long sc in 2nd st to right of last long sc, sk next st on last row, sc in next st, *long sc in center of 4th st from last long sc on 3rd row below, sk next st on last row, sc in next st, long sc in 2nd st to right of last long sc, sk next st on last row, sc in next st; rep from * once more, turn.

Row 8: Ch 1, sc in each st across changing to B, turn.

Rep Rows 1–8 for pattern.

Crisscross Stitch Pullover

Design by Darla Sims

Versatile motion-friendly styling makes this sweater a comfortable choice for young boys or girls. Make it in his or her favorite colors.

 **INTERMEDIATE**

Sizes
8 [10, 12]
Pattern is written for smallest size with changes for larger sizes in brackets.

Finished Chest Measurements
30 [32, 34] inches

Materials
Paton Look At Me sport (fine) weight yarn (152 yds/1¾ oz/50g per ball);
    5 [6, 6] balls #6351 white (A)
    4 [4, 5] balls #6377 fun 'n games (B)
Size E/4/3.5mm crochet hook
Size G/6/4mm crochet hook or size needed to obtain gauge
Yarn needle

Gauge
8 sts = 2 inches

Back
Ribbing
Row 1: With smaller hook and A, ch 11, sc in 2nd ch from hook and in each ch across, turn. *(10 sc)*

Row 2: Ch 1, working in **back lps** *(see Stitch Guide)* only sc in each sc across, turn.

Rows 3–60 [68, 72]: Rep Row 2. Change to larger hook.

Body
Foundation row (RS): Ch 1, working in ends of rows, sc 61 [65, 69] evenly spaced across, changing to B in last sc. Fasten off.

Row 1 (RS): Ch 1, sc in each sc across, turn.

Row 2: Ch 1, sc in each sc across changing to A in last sc, turn.

Row 3: Ch 1, sc in first 3 sc, **long sc** *(see Special Stitches on page 129)* in center of 6th st on 3rd row below, sk next st on last row, sc in next st, long sc in 2nd st to right of last long sc, sk next st on last row, sc in next st; *long sc in 4th st from last long sc, sk next st on last row, sc in next st, long sc in 2nd st to right of last long sc, sk next st on last row, sc in next st; rep from * 12 [13, 14] times more, sc in last 2 sc, turn.

Row 4: Ch 1, sc in each st across changing to B in last sc, turn.

Row 5: Ch 1, sc in each sc across, turn.

Row 6: Ch 1, sc in each sc across changing to A in last sc, turn.

Row 7: Ch 1, sc in first sc, long sc in center of 4th st on 3rd row below, sk next st on last row, sc in next sc, long sc in 2nd st to right of last long sc, sk next st on last row, sc in next st, *long sc in center of 4th st from last long sc on 3rd row below, sk next st on last row, sc in next st, long sc in 2nd st to right of last long sc, sk next st on last row, sc in next st; rep from * 12 [13, 14] times more, turn.

Row 8: Ch 1, sc in each st across changing to B, turn.

Rep Rows 1–8 until piece measures 11 [13, 15] inches.
Place markers at each end of last row to mark armholes.
Continue to work even in established pattern until back measures 17½ [20, 23] inches ending with a WS row.
Fasten off.

Front
Work as for back until armhole measures 4 [5, 6] inches, ending with a WS row.

Right neck shaping
*Note: For **sc dec**, pull up lp in each of next 2 sts, yo, draw through all 3 lps on hook.*

Row 1 (RS): Ch 1, work in pattern across 22 [24, 25] sts, turn, leaving rem sts unworked.

Row 2: Ch 1, work in pattern across, turn.

Row 3: Ch 1, work in pattern to last 2 sts, sc dec, turn. *(21, 23, 24 sts)*

[Rep Rows 2 and 3] 3 times. *(18, 20, 21 sts)*
Work even until same length as back.
Fasten off.

Left neck shaping
Row 1 (RS): With RS facing, sk next 17 [17, 19] sts from right neck, attach yarn in next st with sl st, ch 1, sc in same st, work in pattern across, turn. *(22, 24, 25 sts)*

Row 2: Ch 1, work in pattern across, turn.

Row 3: Ch 1, sc dec, work in pattern across, turn. *(21, 23, 24 sts)*

[Rep Rows 2 and 3] 3 times more. *(18, 20, 21 sts)*
Work even until same length as back.

Sleeves
Ribbing
Row 1: With smaller hook and A, ch 11, sc in 2nd ch from hook and in each ch across, turn. *(10 sc)*

Row 2: Ch 1, working in **back lps** only sc in each sc across, turn.

Rows 3–28 [30, 32]: Rep Row 2.
Change to larger hook.

Body
Foundation row (RS): Ch 1, working along side of ribbing in ends of rows, sc 37 [41, 45] evenly spaced across, changing to B in last sc. Fasten off.

Row 1 (RS): Ch 1, sc in each sc across, turn.

Row 2: Ch 1, sc in each sc across changing to A in last sc, turn.

Row 3: Ch 1, sc in first 3 sc, long sc in center of 6th st on 3rd row below, sk next st on last row, sc in next st, long sc in 2nd st to right of last long sc, sk next st on last row, sc in next st; *long sc in 4th st from last long sc, sk next st on last row, sc in next st, long sc in 2nd st to right of last long sc, sk next st on last row, sc in next st; rep from * 6 [7, 8] times more, sc in last 2 sc, turn.

Row 4: Ch 1, 2 sc in first st *(inc)* sc in each st to last st, 2 sc in last st *(inc)* changing to B in last sc, turn. *(39, 43, 47 sc)*

Continued on page 142

Popcorn Stripe Stitch

Popcorns made with single crochets and front post double crochets form the basis in creating this interesting textural stitch.

Knit

Crochet

Crochet Stitch Pattern

Special Stitches

For **popcorn (pc),** 5 sc in st indicated, remove lp from hook, insert hook in first dc, pull dropped lp through.

For **front post double crochet (fpdc),** yo, insert hook from front to back around post *(see Stitch Guide)* of st indicated, yo, draw lp through, [yo, draw through 2 lps on hook] 2 times. **Note:** *Sk st behind fpdc on last row.*

Multiple of 8 sts + 4

Row 1 (RS): Ch 22, sc in 2nd ch from hook and in each ch across, turn. *(21 sc)*

Row 2 & all even-numbered rows: Ch 1, sc in each st across, turn.

Row 3: Ch 1, sc in first sc, *__pc__ *(see Special Stitches)* in next sc, sc in next 3 sc, **fpdc** *(see Special Stitches)* around 6th sc on row before last, sk next st on last row, sc in next 3 sc; rep from * once more, pc in next st, sc in next sc, turn.

Row 5: Ch 1, sc in first sc, *pc in next sc, sc in next 3 sc, fpdc around next fpdc, sc in next 3 sc; rep from * once more, pc in next st, sc in next sc, turn.

Row 7: Rep Row 5.

Row 9: Ch 1, sc in first sc, *fpdc around top of pc on row before last, sc in next 3 sc, pc in next sc, sc in next 3 sc; rep from * once more, fpdc around top of next pc on row before last, sc in next sc, turn.

Row 11: Ch 1, sc in first sc, *fpdc around next fpdc, sc in next 3 sc, pc in next sc, sc in next 3 sc; rep from * once more, fpdc around next fpdc, sc in next sc, turn.

Popcorn Stripe Stitch Pullover

Design by Darla Sims

Comfortable to wear and sized both for young children and cuddly teddy bears, what child wouldn't love having the same sweater as their furry buddy?

◼◼◻◻ **EASY**

Sizes
2 [4, 6]
Pattern is written for smallest size with changes for larger sizes in brackets.

Finished Chest Measurements
25 [27, 29] inches

Materials
Brown Sheep Lamb's Pride Superwash medium (worsted) weight yarn (200 yds/3½ oz/100g per ball); 5 [5, 6] balls #SW35 sweeten pink
Note: Yarn sufficient for both child and teddy sweaters
Size G/6/4mm crochet hook
Size H/8/5mm crochet hook or size needed to obtain gauge
Yarn needle
16-inch teddy bear with 14-inch waist

Gauge
With larger hook: 7 sts = 2 inches

Back
Row 1 (RS): With larger hook, ch 44 [48, 52], sc in 2nd ch from hook and in each ch across, turn. *(43, 47, 51 sc)*

Row 13: Rep Row 11.

Row 14: Ch 1, sc in each st across, turn.

Rep Rows 3–14 for pattern.

Row 2 & all even-numbered rows: Ch 1, sc in each st across, turn.

Row 3: Ch 1, sc in first 1 [3, 5] sc, ***pc** *(see Special Stitches on page 133)* in next sc, sc in next 3 sc, **fpdc** *(see Special Stitches on page 133)* around 6th sc on row before last, sk next st on last row, sc in next 3 sc; rep from * 4 times more, pc in next st, sc in next 1 [3, 5] sc, turn.

Row 5: Ch 1, sc in first 1 [3, 5] sc, *pc in next sc, sc in next 3 sc, fpdc around next fpdc, sc in next 3 sc; rep from * 4 times more, pc in next st, sc in next 1 [3, 5] sc, turn.

Row 7: Rep Row 5.

Row 9: Ch 1, sc in first 1 [3, 5] sc, *fpdc around top of pc on row before last, sc in next 3 sc, pc in next sc, sc in next 3 sc; rep from * once more, fpdc around top of next pc on row before last, sc in next 1 [3, 5] sc, turn.

Row 11: Ch 1, sc in first 1 [3, 5] sc, *fpdc around next fpdc, sc in next 3 sc, pc in next sc, sc in next 3 sc; rep from * once more, fpdc around next fpdc, sc in next 1 [3, 5] sc, turn.

Row 13: Rep Row 11.

Row 14: Ch 1, sc in each st across, turn.
Rep Rows 3–14 until piece measures 8 [9, 10] inches. Place markers at each end of last row for armholes.
Continue in pattern until piece measures 13 [14½, 15½] inches, ending with a RS row.
Fasten off.

Front
Work as for back until armhole measures 2 [2, 2½] inches less than back, ending with a WS row.

Right neck shaping
*Note: For **sc dec**, pull up lp in each of next 2 sts, yo, draw through all 3 lps on hook.*

Row 1 (RS): Ch 1, work in pattern across 17 [18, 19] sts, turn, leaving rem sts unworked.

Row 2: Ch 1, **sc dec** *(see Note),* work in pattern across, turn. *(16, 17, 18 sts)*

Row 3: Ch 1, work in pattern across, turn.
[Rep Rows 1 and 2] 3 times. *(13, 14, 15 sts)*
Work even in pattern until piece is same length as back.
Fasten off.

Left neck shaping
Row 1 (RS): With RS facing, sk next 9 [11, 13] sts, attach yarn with sl st in next st, ch 1, sc in same st, work in pattern across, turn.

Row 2: Ch 1, work in pattern to last 2 sts, sc dec, turn.

Row 3: Ch 1, work in pattern across.
[Rep Rows 2 and 3] 3 times. *(13, 14, 15 sts)*
Work even in pattern until piece is same length as right neck.
Fasten off.

Sleeves
Row 1 (RS): With larger hook, ch 24 [26, 28], sc in 2nd ch from hook and in each ch across, turn. *(23, 25, 27 sc)*

Row 2: Ch 1, sc in each sc across, turn.

Row 3: Ch 1, sc in first 3 [4, 5] sc, *pc in next st, sc in next 3 sc, sk first 7 [8, 9] sc on row before last, fpdc around next sc, sk next sc on last row, sc in next 3 sc; rep from * once more, pc in next sc, sc in next 3 [4, 5] sc, turn.

Row 4: Ch 1, sc in each sc across, turn.
Note: Pattern is worked over center 17 sts, sts on each side of pattern are worked as sc on each row.

Row 5: Ch 1, sc in first 3 [4, 5] sc, *pc in next st, sc in next 3 sc, fpdc around next fpdc, sc in next 3 sc; rep from * once more, pc in next sc, sc in next 3 [4, 5] sc, turn.

Row 6: Ch 1, 2 sc in first sc *(inc)*, sc in next 2 [3, 4] sc, *pc in next st, sc in next 3 sts, fpdc around next fpdc, sc in next 3 sc; rep from * once more, pc in next sc, sc in next 2 [3, 4] sc, 2 sc in next sc *(inc)*, turn. *(25, 27, 29 sts)*
Continue to work in pattern as established, inc 1 st, each end, every 6th row 5 [6, 6] times more. *(35, 39, 41 sts)*
Work even in pattern until sleeve measures 9 [10½, 11½] inches or desired length, ending with a WS row. Fasten off.

Finishing
Sew shoulder seams. Matching center of sleeve to shoulder seam and edges of sleeves to markers, sew in sleeves. Sew sleeve and side as 1 continuous seam.

Edgings
Sleeve edging
With RS facing and smaller hook, attach yarn to 1 sleeve seam, ch 1, sc in same st, sc around keeping edge flat; join with sl st. Fasten off.
Rep for other sleeve.

Lower edging

With RS facing and smaller hook, attach yarn side seam, ch 1, sc in same st, sc around lower edge keeping edge flat; join with sl st. Fasten off.

Neck edging

Rnd 1: With RS facing and smaller hook, attach yarn to 1 shoulder seam, ch 1, sc in same st, sc around neck, working sc dec at each corner of neck; join with sl st in first sc.

Rnd 2: Ch 1, sc in same st as joining, pc in next sc, *sc in next sc, pc in next sc; rep from * around adjusting as necessary to end with pc; join in first sc.
Fasten off.

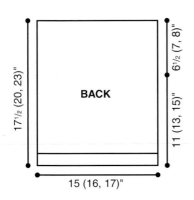

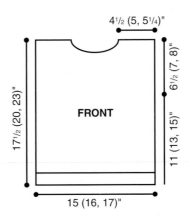

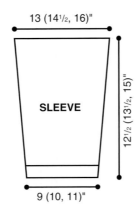

Teddy Bear Sweater

Back

Row 1 (RS): With larger hook, ch 24, sc in 2nd ch from hook and in each ch across, turn. *(23 sc)*

Row 2: Ch 1, sc in each sc across, turn.

Row 3: Ch 1, sc in first 3 sc, ***pc** (see Special Stitches on page 133)* in next st, sc in next 3 sc, sk next 7 sc on row before last, **fpdc** *(see Special Stitches on page 133)* around next sc, sk next sc on last row, sc in next 3 sc; rep from * once more, pc in next sc, sc in next 3 sc, turn.

Row 4: Ch 1, sc in each sc across, turn.

Row 5: Ch 1, sc in first 3 sc, *pc in next st, sc in next 3 sc, fpdc around next fpdc, sc in next 3 sc; rep from * once more, pc in next sc, sc in next 3 sc, turn.

Rows 6 & 7: Rep Rows 4 and 5.

Row 8: Rep Row 4.

Sleeves

Row 1 (RS): Ch 7, sc in 2nd ch from hook and in next 8 sts, *fpdc around top of next pc, sc in next 3 sc, pc in next sc, sc in next 3 sc; rep from * once more, fpdc around top of next pc, sc in next 3 sc, turn.

Row 2: Ch 7, sc in 2nd ch from hook and in each st across, turn. *(35 sts)*

Rows 3–14: Work in pattern as established across center 17 sts, work sts on each side of pattern in sc.
Fasten off.

Front

Work as for back to sleeves.

Sleeve & right neck

Row 1 (RS): Ch 7, sc in 2nd ch from hook and in next 8 sts, *fpdc around top of next pc, sc in next 3 sc, pc in next sc, sc in next 3 sc; rep from * once more, fpdc around top of next pc, sc in next 3 sc, turn.

Row 2: Ch 7, sc in 2nd ch from hook and in each st across, turn.

Row 3: Ch 1, sc in first 9 sc, *fpdc around next fpdc, sc in next 3 sc, pc in next sc, sc in next 3 sc; rep from * once more, fpdc around next fpdc, sc in next 9 sc, turn.

Row 4: Ch 1, sc in each st across, turn.

Rows 5 & 6: Rep Rows 3 and 4.

Row 7: Ch 1, sc in first 10 sts, turn, leaving rem sts unworked.

Row 8: Ch 1, sc in each st across, turn.
Rep Row 8 until same length as back.
Fasten off.

Sleeve & left neck

Row 1 (RS): With RS facing, sk next 15 sts from right front, attach yarn in next st with sl st, ch 1, sc in same st and in next 9 sc, turn. *(10 sc)*

Row 2: Ch 1, sc in each st across, turn.
Rep Row 2 until same length as right neck.
Fasten off.

Finishing

Sew shoulder seams. Sew sleeve and side seam as 1 continuous seam.

Edgings
Sleeve edging
With RS facing and smaller hook, attach

yarn to 1 sleeve seam, ch 1, sc in same st, sc around keeping edge flat; join with sl st.
Fasten off.
Rep for other sleeve.

Lower edging

With RS facing and smaller hook, attach yarn in 1 side seam, ch 1, sc in same st, sc around lower edge keeping edge flat; join with sl st.
Fasten off.

Neck edging

Rnd 1: With RS facing and smaller hook, attach yarn in 1 shoulder seam, ch 1, sc in same st, sc around neck, working sc dec at each corner of neck; join with sl st in first sc.

Rnd 2: Ch 1, sc in same st as joining, pc in next sc, *sc in next sc, pc in next sc; rep from * around adjusting as necessary to end with pc; join in first sc.
Fasten off. ♣

Cherry Clusters & Zigzag Duster
Continued from 114

fpdc and top of next pc, sk next 3 sts on last row, sc in each rem st across, turn.

Row 11: Ch 1, sc in first 13 [13, 15, 15, 16] sc, 3-fpdc cl, over next 3 fpdc, sk next st on last row, sc in each rem st across, turn.

Row 12: Ch 1, sc in each st across, turn.

Row 13: Ch 1, bpsc in each st across, turn.

Row 14: Ch 1, 2 sc in first st *(inc),* sc in each st to last st, 2 sc in last st *(inc),* turn. *(29, 29, 31, 31, 33 sts)*

Row 15: Ch 1, sc in each st across, turn.

Row 16: Ch 1, sc in each st across, turn.
[Rep Rows 14–16] 14 [16, 16, 18, 18] times. *(57, 61, 63, 67, 69 sts)*

Rep Row 16 until sleeve measures 17 [17½, 17¾, 18, 18¼] inches or desired length.
Fasten off.

Finishing

Sew shoulder seams. Sew sleeve seams. Sew sleeves in armhole opening matching center top of sleeve to shoulder seam and underarm seam with skipped sts.

Edging

Hold piece with RS facing and lower-edge at top, attach yarn in first sc, ch 1, sc in same st, sc around entire outer edge working 3 sc in each lower-edge corner and spacing sc to keep piece flat; join with sl st in first sc.
Fasten off.

Ties

With smallest hook, attach yarn at beg of V shaping of 1 front, ch 40.
Fasten off.
Rep for other front. ♣

Raised Zigzag Top
Continued from 118

[Rep last 2 rows] 5 times more. *(9, 10, 11, 12 sts)* Work even in pattern until armhole measures same as back.
Fasten off.

Finishing
Sew shoulder and side seams.

Edgings
Armhole edging
Rnd 1: With RS facing and smaller hook, attach A with sl st at one underarm seam, ch 1, sc in same st, sc around armhole, keeping work flat, join with sl st.

Rnd 2: Ch 1, sc in same st as joining and in each sc around, join.
Fasten off.

Rep for other armhole.

Neck edging
Rnd 1: With RS facing and smaller hook, attach A in one shoulder seam, ch 1, sc in same st, sc around, working 3 sc in each corner and keeping work flat, join with sl st in first sc.

Rnd 2: Ch 1, sc in same st as joining and in each sc around, join.
Fasten off.

Lower edging
With RS facing and smaller hook, attach A to any st directly below long sc, ch 1, sc in same st, *ch 5, sc in 2nd ch from hook, hdc in next ch, dc in next ch, tr in last ch, sk next 3 sts on lower edge; rep from * around, join. Fasten off. ❧

Lattice Cables Tunic
Continued from 123

Work even until sleeve measures 17 inches.
Fasten off.

For **sizes medium and large** only, rep Row 2, inc 1 st, each end every other row 2 times, then inc 1 st, each end, every 4th row 15 [16] times. *(66, 70 sts)*

Work even until sleeve measures 17½ [17½] inches.
Fasten off.

For **sizes extra-large and 2X-large** only, rep Row 2, inc 1 st, each end every other row 3 times, then inc 1 st, each edge, every 4th row 14 [15] times. *(74, 78 sts)*

Work even until sleeve measures 17¾ [18] inches.
Fasten off.

Finishing
Sew shoulder seams. Set in sleeves. Sew sleeve and side in one continuous seam, leaving 3 inches open at bottom of each side for slit.

Edging
Neck edging
*Note: For **sc dec**, pull up lp in each of next 2 sts, yo and draw through all 3 lps on hook.*

Rnd 1 (RS): With RS facing, attach yarn in 1 shoulder seam, ch 1, sc in same st, sc around, working **sc dec** *(see Note)* at each corner, join with sl st in first sc.

Rnd 2: Ch 1, working from left to right reverse sc *(see Stitch Guide)* in each st around, join.
Fasten off.

Lower edging
Rnd 1 (RS): With RS facing, attach yarn in 1 side seam, ch 1, sc in same st, sc around, working 3 sc in each outer corner, join with sl st in first sc.

Rnd 2: Ch 1, working from left to right reverse sc in each st around, join.
Fasten off.

Sleeve edging
Rnd 1 (RS): With RS facing, attach yarn in 1 sleeve seam, ch 1, sc in same st, sc around, join with sl st in first sc.

Rnd 2: Ch 1, working from left to right rev sc in each st around, join.
Fasten off.
Rep for other sleeve. ❖

Knotted Cables Vest
Continued from 128

V-neck edging
*Note: For **3-sc dec**, pull up lp in each of next 3 sts, yo, draw through all 4 lps on hook.*

Rnd 1: With RS facing and smaller hook, attach yarn to shoulder seam, ch 1, sc in same st, sc around neck edge, keeping edge flat; join with sl st in first st. Mark center front st.

Rnd 2: Ch 1, sc in same st as joining and in each sc to st before marker, **3-sc dec** *(see Note)* over next 3 sts, sc in each rem sc, join in first sc. Fasten off. ❖

Crisscross Stitch Pullover
Continued from 132

Row 5: Ch 1, sc in each sc across, turn.

Row 6: Ch 1, sc in each sc across changing to A in last sc, turn.

Row 7: Ch 1, sc in 2 sc, long sc in center of 4th st on 3rd row below, sk next st on last row, sc in next sc, long sc in 2nd st to right of last long sc, sk next st on last row, sc in next st, *long sc in center of 4th st from last long sc on 3rd row below, sk next st on last row, sc in next st, long sc in 2nd st to right of last long sc, sk next st on last row, sc in next 2 sts; rep from * 6 [7, 8] times more, turn.

Row 8: Ch 1, 2 sc in first st, sc in each st to last st, 2 sc in last st changing to B, turn. *(41, 45, 49 sts)*
Continue in pattern as established inc 1 st each edge every 4th row 6 [7, 8] times more. *(53, 59, 65 sts)*
Work even in pattern until sleeve measures 12½ [13½, 15] inches.
Fasten off.

Finishing
Sew shoulder seams. Matching center of sleeve to shoulder seam and edges of sleeves to markers, sew in sleeves. Sew sleeve and side seams as 1 continuous seam.

Neck Edging
Rnd 1: With RS facing and smaller hook, attach A at 1 shoulder seam, ch 1, sc in same st, sc around keeping edge flat; join with sl st in first sc.

Rnd 2: Ch 1, sc in same st as joining and in each sc around, join changing to B.

Rnd 3: Ch 1, sc in same st as joining and in each sc around, join changing to A.

Rnd 4: Ch 1, sc in same st as joining and in each sc around, join.

Rnd 5: Rep Rnd 4.
Fasten off. ❧

Chapter 6
Accessories

You'll find fashionable hats, stunning scarves and fun-to-use purses in this delightful collection. Try a new stitch pattern as you create these wearable treats.

Brick Wall

Single crochet stripes are accented with long alternating single crochets that form the "mortar" between the "bricks."

Knit

Crochet

Crochet Stitch Pattern

Note: Pattern stitch is worked in 2 colors (A and B).

Special Stitch

   For long single crochet (long sc), pull up lp in st indicated on row below, pull up to height of row being worked, yo, draw through 2 lps on hook.

Multiple of 17 sts + 1
Note: Pattern is worked on RS only.

Row 1 (RS): With B, ch 18, sc in 2nd ch from hook and in each rem ch. Fasten off. *(17 sc)*

Row 2: Join B in first sc of Row 1; ch 1, sc in each sc. Fasten off.

Row 3: Join A in first sc of Row 2; ch 1, sc in first 2 sc, [ch 1, sk next sc, sc in next 5 sc] 2 times, ch 1, sk next sc, sc in next 2 sc. Fasten off.

Row 4: Join A in first sc of Row 3; ch 1, sc in each sc and in each ch-1 sp. Fasten off.

Row 5: Join B in first sc of Row 4; ch 1, sc in first 2 sc, **long sc** *(see Special Stitch)* in next skipped sc on row before last, sc in next 5 sc, long sc in next skipped sc on row before last, sc in next 5 sc, long sc in next skipped sc on row before last, sc in next 2 sc. Fasten off.

Row 6: Join B in first sc of Row 5; ch 1, sc in each sc. Fasten off.

Row 7: Join A in first sc of Row 6; ch 1, sc in

first 5 sc, [ch 1, sk next sc, sc in next 5 sc] 2 times. Fasten off.

Row 8: Join A in first sc of Row 7; ch 1, sc in each sc. Fasten off.

Row 9: Join B in first sc of Row 8; ch 1, sc in first 5 sc, long sc in next skipped sc on row before last, sc in next 5 sc, long sc in next skipped sc on row before last, sc in next 5 sc. Fasten off.

Row 10: Join B in first sc of Row 9; ch 1, sc in each sc. Fasten off.

Rep Rows 3–10 for pattern.

Brick Wall Cloche

Design by Darla Sims

This versatile style with be appreciated by all ages when the weather turns crisp and the wind chills the bones. This hat may be made in any favorite shade of worsted weight yarn.

 **INTERMEDIATE**

Finished Size
One size fits most

Materials
Lion Brand Wool-Ease medium (worsted) weight yarn:
    3 oz/197 yds/85g
        #124 caramel (A)
    3 oz/197 yds/85g
        #099 fisherman (B)
Size H/8/5mm or size needed to obtain gauge

Gauge
7 sts = 2 inches

Top Section
With A, loosely ch 2.

Note: *Top section is worked in continuous rnds, do not join unless instructed. Mark beg of rnds.*

Rnd 1: 8 sc in 2nd ch from hook.

Rnd 2: 2 sc in each sc. *(16 sc)*

Rnd 3: [Sc in next sc, 2 sc in next sc] 8 times. *(24 sc)*

Rnd 4: [Sc in next 2 sc, 2 sc in next sc] 8 times. *(32 sc)*

Rnd 5: [Sc in next 3 sc, 2 sc in next sc] 8 times. *(40 sc)*

Rnd 6: [Sc in next 4 sc, 2 sc in next sc] 8 times. *(48 sc)*

Rnd 7: [Sc in next 5 sc, 2 sc in next sc] 8 times. *(56 sc)*

Rnd 8: [Sc in next 6 sc, 2 sc in next sc] 8 times. *(64 sc)*

Rnd 9: Sc in each sc.

Rep Rnd 9 until piece measures 3½ inches from beg. At end of last rnd, join in first sc. Fasten off.

Center Section
Rnd 1: Join B in first sc; ch 1, sc in same sc and in each rem sc, join in first sc.

Rnd 2: Ch 1, sc in same sc and in each rem sc, join in first sc. Change to A by drawing lp through; cut B.

Continued on page 156

Bobbled Arrows

The arrows are formed with long single crochet stitches with the point of each arrow neatly detailed with a bobble popcorn stitch.

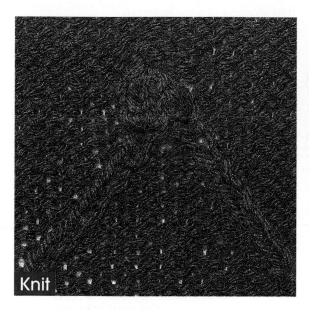
Knit

Crochet

Crochet Stitch Pattern

Special Stitches

For **long single crochet** (**long sc**), pull up lp in sp or st indicated on row below to height of working row, yo, draw through 2 lps on hook.

For **popcorn** (**pc**), 5 dc in st indicated, remove lp from hook, insert hook in first dc made and draw dropped lp through.

Multiple of 14 sts + 1
Note: *Pattern is worked on RS only.*

Row 1 (RS): Loosely ch 15, sc in 2nd ch from hook and in each rem ch. Fasten off. *(12 sc)*

Rows 2–4: Join in first sc of previous row, ch 1, sc in same sc and in each rem sc. Fasten off.

Row 5: Join in first sc of Row 4; ch 1, sc in first 2 sc, **long sc** *(see Special Stitches)* in sc directly below first sc on row below last; sc in next 7 sc on last row; sk next 9 sc from long sc on row below last, long sc in next sc, on last row, sc in next 3 sc. Fasten off.

Row 6 & all even-numbered rows: Join in first sc of previous row; ch 1, sc in each rem sc. Fasten off.

Row 7: Join in first sc of previous row; ch 1, sc in first 4 sc, long sc in next long sc on row below last, sc in next 5 sc, long sc in next long sc on row below last, sc in next 3 sc. Fasten off.

Row 9: Join in first sc of previous row; ch 1, sc in first 6 sc, long sc in next long sc on row below last, sc in next 3 sc, long sc in next long sc on row below last, sc in next 3 sc. Fasten off.

Row 11: Join in first sc of previous row; ch 1, sc in same sc and in next 7 sc, long sc in next long sc on row below last, sc in next sc, long sc in next long sc on row below last,

sc in next 3 sc. Fasten off.

Row 13: Join in first sc of previous row, ch 1, sc in first 8 sc, **pc** *(see Special Stitches on page 147)* around sc below next sc on row below last; sc in next 5 sc. Fasten off.

Rep Rows 2–13 for pattern.

Bobbled Arrows Hat

Design by Darla Sims

Made in the round without joining the rows, all ages will enjoy wearing this warm and comfy style hat.

 **EASY**

Finished Size
One size fits most

Materials
Lion Brand Wool-Ease medium (worsted) weight yarn: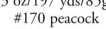
   3 oz/197 yds/85g
     #170 peacock
Size H/8/5mm or size needed to obtain gauge
Size G/6/4mm
Yarn needle

Gauge
With larger hook, 7 sts = 2 inches

Hat
With larger hook, loosely ch 60; join to form a ring, taking care not to twist ch.

Rnd 1: Ch 1, sc in same ch as joining and in each rem ch, join with sl st in first sc.

Rnds 2–4: Ch 1, sc in same sc as joining and in each rem sc, join with sl st in first sc.

Rnd 5: Ch 1, sc in same sc as joining and in next sc, **long sc** *(see Special Stitches on page 147)* in sc directly below first sc on row

below last, *sc in next 7 sc on last row, sk next 9 sc from long sc on row below last, long sc in next sc on last row, sc in next 3 sc; sk next sc from long sc on row below last, long sc in next sc; rep from * 3 times more, sc in next 7 sc on last row, sk next 9 sc from long sc on row below last, long sc in next sc, on last row, sc in next 3 sc, join with sl st in first sc.

Rnd 6 & all even-numbered rnds: Ch 1, sc in same sc and in each rem sc.

Rnd 7: Ch 1, sc in same sc and in next 3 sc, *long sc in next long sc, sc in next 5 sc, long sc in next long sc on row below last, sc in next 5 sc; rep from * 3 times more, long sc in next long sc, sc in next 5 sc, long sc in next long sc on row below last, sc in next sc, join with sl st in first sc.

Rnd 9: Ch 1, sc in same sc and in next 5 sc, *long sc in next long sc, sc in next 3 sc, long sc in next long sc, sc in next 7 sc; rep from * 3 times more, long sc in next long sc, sc in next sc, join with sl st in first sc.

Rnd 11: Ch 1, sc in same sc, sc in next 7 sc, *long sc in next long sc, sc in next sc, long sc in next long sc, sc in next 9 sc; rep from

* 4 times more, long sc in next long sc, sc in next sc, join with sl st in first sc.

Rnd 13: Ch 1, sc in first 9 sc, ***pc** (see Special Stitches on page 147)* around sc below next sc on row below last; sc in next 7 sc; rep from * 3 times more, pc around sc below next sc on row below, last sc in next 4 sc, join with sl st in first sc. Turn.
Note: *Rem of hat is worked in continuous rnds; do not join. Mark beg of rnds.*

Rnd 14: Ch 1, sc in each sc.

Rnd 15: Sc in each sc.
Rep Rnd 15 until piece measures 6½ inches from beg.
Note: *For sc dec, pull up lp in next 2 sts, yo and draw through all 3 lps on hook.*

Working in continuous rnds, *sc in next 4 sc, **sc dec** (see Note); rep from * for 1½ inches.

Continuing in continuous rnds, *sc in next 3 sc, sc dec; rep from * for 1 inch.

Next 2 rnds: Sc in each sc.

Point of Hat
*Sc in next 2 sc, sc dec; rep from * until 5 sc rem. Cut yarn and draw top sts tog. Pull end through to WS and weave in.

Lower Edging
With smaller hook, join with a sl st in first unused lp of beg ch; ch 1, sc in same lp and in each rem unused lp; join with sl st in first sc.
Fasten off. ❖

Lobster Claw

*Created with an ingenious combination of front post double crochets,
this stitch offers interesting texture and uniqueness.*

Knit

Crochet

Crochet Stitch Pattern

Special Stitch

For front post double crochet (fpdc), yo,
insert hook from front to back around **post**
(see Stitch Guide) of st indicated, yo, draw lp
through, [yo, draw through 2 lps on hook] 2
times. ***Note:*** *Sk st behind fpdc on working row.*

Multiple of 10 sts + 1

Row 1 (RS): Loosely ch 11, sc in 2nd ch
from hook and in each rem ch, turn. (10 sc)

Row 2 & all even-numbered rows: Ch 1,
sc in each sc, turn.

Row 3: Ch 1, sc in first sc, **fpdc** *(see Special
Stitch)* around sc below next sc, sc in 6 next sc,
fpdc around sc below next sc, sc in next sc, turn.

Row 5: Ch 1, sc in first sc, fpdc around next
fpdc, fpdc around sc below next sc, sc in
next 4 sc, fpdc around sc below next sc, fpdc
around next fpdc, sc in next sc, turn.

Row 7: Ch 1, sc in first sc, fpdc around each
of next 2 fpdc, sc in next 4 sc, fpdc around
each of next 2 fpdc, sc in next sc, turn.

Row 9: Ch 1, sc in first 3 sc, sk first 2 fpdc,
fpdc around each of next 2 fpdc, fpdc
around each of 2 skipped fpdc, sc in next
3 sts, turn.

Rows 10 & 11: Rep Row 2.

Rep Rows 2–11 for pattern.

Lobster Claw Hat

Design by Darla Sims

A bulky yarn shows off the captivating claw pattern and makes it easy to crochet this hat in a hurry.

 **INTERMEDIATE**

Finished Size
One size fits most

Materials
Lion Brand Kool Wool light weight bulky (worsted) weight yarn:
  10½ oz/360 yds/300g
    #146 fuchsia
Size J/10/6mm or size needed to obtain gauge

Gauge
5 sts = 2 inches

Crown
Rnd 1: Ch 2, 16 sc in first ch, join in first sc.

Rnd 2: Ch 6 (counts as a dc and a ch-3 sp), *sk next sc, dc in next st, ch 3; rep from * 6 times more, join with sl st in 3rd ch of beg ch-6.

Rnd 3: (Sc, hdc, 5 dc, hdc, sc) in each ch-3 sp, join with sl st in first sc.

Rnd 4: Ch 4 (counts as a dc and a ch-1 sp), *sk next 3 sts, dc in next 3 sts, ch 1; rep from * around, join with sl st in 3rd ch of beg ch-4.

Rnd 5: Sc in each st, join with sl st in first sc. (48 sc) Fasten off.

Sides
Row 1: Loosely ch 51, sc in 2nd ch from hook and in each rem ch, turn. (50 sc)

Row 2: Ch 1, sc in each sc, turn.

Rows 3–6: Rep Row 2.

Row 7: Ch 1, sc in next sc, ***fpdc** (see Special Stitch on page 150) around sc below next sc, sc in 6 next sc, fpdc around sc below next sc, sc in next 2 sc,; rep from * 3 times more; fpdc around sc below next sc, sc in next 6 sc, fpdc around sc below next sc, sc in next sc, turn.

Row 8 & all even-numbered rows: Rep Row 2.

Row 9: Ch 1, sc in next sc, *fpdc around next fpdc, fpdc around sc below next sc, sc in next 4 sc, fpdc around sc below next sc, fpdc around next fpdc, sc in next 2 sc, rep from * 3 times more; sc in next sc, turn.

Row 11: Ch 1, sc in next sc, *fpdc around each of next 2 fpdc, sc in next 4 sc, fpdc around each of next 2 fpdc, sc in next 2 sc, rep from * 3 times more; sc in next sc, turn.

Row 13: Ch 1, sc in next 3 sc, *sk next 2 fpdc, fpdc around each of next 2 fpdc, fpdc around each skipped fpdc, sc in next 6 sc, rep from * 3 times more; sc in next 3 sts, turn.

Rows 14 & 15: Rep Row 2.
Fasten off.

Finishing
Sew back seam. Working through **back lps** only, sew sides to crown, easing to fit.

Brim
Rnd 1: Join in any sc, sc in same sc and in next 8 sc, [2 sc in next sc, sc in next 7 sc] 5 times, 2 sc in next sc. *(56 sc)*

Rnds 2–5: Ch 1, sc in same sc and in each rem sc, join with sl st in first sc.
Fasten off. ❧

Sunburst

These sunbursts are fashioned with ordinary stitches in an innovative manner using bobbles for the sun and fans of yarn for the rays.

Knit

Crochet

Crochet Stitch Pattern

Special Stitch

For popcorn (**pc**), 5 sc in st indicated, remove lp from hook, insert hook in first sc made and draw dropped lp through.

Multiple of 13 sts + 1
Note: *Pattern is worked on RS only.*

Rows 1 (RS): Ch 14, sc in 2nd ch from hook and in each rem ch. Fasten off. *(13 sc)*

Row 2: Join in first sc of previous row, ch 1, sc in each sc. Fasten off.

Rows 3–6: Rep Row 2.

Row 7: Join in first sc of previous row, ch 1, sc in first 6 sc, yo, insert hook 5 rows below, 5 sps to right, yo and pull up lp to height of working row, [sk next sp, pull up lp in next sp] 4 times; yo and draw through all 6 lps on hook, ch 1, sc in next 6 sc. Fasten off.

Row 8: Join in first sc of previous row, ch 1, sc in first 6 sc, **pc** *(see Special Stitch)* in next st, sc in next 6 sc. Fasten off.

Row 9: Join in first sc of previous row, ch 1, sc in each sc. Fasten off.

Rep Rows 2–9 for pattern.

Sunburst Mittens

Design by Darla Sims

A trio of sunbursts dresses up the backs of our fashionable sport weight mittens. Made in a lively mango color, they will brighten even the grayest winter day.

 INTERMEDIATE

Finished Size
One size fits most

Materials
Patons Astra fine (sport) weight yarn
   3½ oz/266 yds/100g
      #8714 mango
Size H/8/5mm or size needed to obtain gauge
Size G/6/4mm
Yarn needle

4 MEDIUM

Gauge
4 sts = 1 inch

Right Mitten
Note: Mittens are worked in continuous rnds, do not join unless instructed. Mark beg of rnds.

With larger hook, ch 2.

Rnd 1: 8 sc in 2nd ch from hook.

Rnd 2: 2 sc in each sc. *(16 sc)*

Rnd 3: [Sc in next sc, 2 sc in next sc] 8 times. *(24 sc)*

Rnd 4: [Sc in next 2 sc, 2 sc in next sc] 8 times. *(32 sc)*

Rnd 5: Sc in 16 sc, 2 sc in next sc, sc in next 15 sc. *(33 sc)*

Rnds 6: Sc in each sc.

Rnds 7–14: Sc in each sc.

Rnd 15: Sc in next 16 sc, yo, insert hook 5 rows below, 5 sps to right, yo and pull up lp to height of working row, [sk next sp, pull up lp in next sp] 4 times; yo and draw through all 6 lps on hook, ch 1, sc in next 16 sc.

Rnd 16: Sc in next 16 sc, **pc** *(see Special Stitch on page 153)* in next st, sc in next 16 sc.

Rnds 17–22: Rep Rnd 6.

Rnd 23: Rep Rnd 15.

Rnd 24: Ch 5, sk next 5 sc, sc in next 11 sc, pc in next st, sc in next 16 sc.

Rnd 25: Sc in each sc and in each ch.

Rnds 26–30: Rep Rnd 6.

Rnds 31 & 32: Rep Rnds 15 and 16.

Rnds 33 & 34: Rep Rnd 6.

Ribbing
Change to smaller hook and ch 13.

Row 1: Sc in back lp only of 2nd ch from hook and in each ch, sl st in next 2 sc on piece, turn.

Row 2: Ch 1, sk next 2 sl sts, sc in back lp of next 12 sc, turn.

Row 3: Ch 1, sc in back lp of next 12 sc, sl st in next 2 sc on piece.

[Rep Rows 2 and 3] 10 times more.

Next row: Rep Row 2.

Next row: Ch 1, sc in back lp of next 12 sc. Do not fasten off.

Working in **back lps** only, sl st first and last rows of ribbing tog.

Fasten off.

Thumb

Rnd 1: With larger hook, join in first skipped sc on Rnd 23, ch 1, sc in same sc and in next 4 skipped sc, working in unused lps of ch-5 sp of Rnd 24, sc in each lp, join with sl st in first sc.

Rnds 2–8: Ch 1, sc in same sc and in each rem sc; join with sl st in first sc.

Rnd 9: Pull up lp in same sc and in each of next 2 sc, yo and draw through all 4 lps on hook, [pull up lp in next 3 sc, yo and draw through all 4 lps on hook] 3 times; join with a sl st in first st. Fasten off.

Left Mitten

With larger hook, ch 2.

Rnds 1–23: Rep Rnds 1–23 of right mitten.

Rnd 24: Sc in next 16 sc, **pc** *(see Special Stitch on page 153)* in next st, sc in next 11 sc, ch 5, sk last 5 sc.

Rnds 25–34: Rep Rnds 25–34 of right mitten.

Ribbing

Work same as ribbing for right mitten.

Thumb

Work same as thumb for right mitten.

Finishing

Sew opening at top of each thumb closed. ❧

Brick Wall Cloche
Continued from 146

Rnd 3: Ch 1, sc in same sc and in next sc, *ch 1, sk next sc, sc in next 5 sc; rep from * 9 times more, ch 1, sk next sc, sc in next 2 sc, join in first sc.

Rnd 4: Ch 1, sc in same sc, in each rem sc and in each ch-1 sp, join in first sc. Change to B; cut A.

Rnd 5: Ch 1, sc in same sc and in next sc, **long sc** *(see Special Stitch on page 144)* in next skipped sc on row before last, sc in next 5 sc; *long sc in next skipped sc on row before last, sc in next 5 sc; rep from * 9 times more, long sc in next skipped sc on row before last, sc in next 2 sc, join in first sc.

Rnd 6: Ch 1, sc in same sc and in each rem sc, join in first sc. Change to A; cut B.

Rnd 7: Ch 1, sc in same sc and in next 4 sc, *ch 1, sk next sc, sc in next 5 sc; rep from * 9 times more, ch 1, sk next sc, sc in next 4 sc, ch 1, sk next sc, sc in next sc, join in first sc.

Rnd 8: Ch 1, sc in same sc, in each rem sc and in each ch-1 sp, join in first sc. Change to B; cut A.

Rnd 9: Ch 1, sc in same sc and in next 4 sc, *long sc in next skipped sc on row before last, sc in next 5 sc; rep from * 9 times more, long sc in next skipped sc on row before last, sc in next sc, join in first sc.

Rnd 10: Ch 1, sc in same sc and in each rem sc, join in first sc. Change to A; cut B.

Rnds 11–14: Rep Rnds 3–6.

Rnd 15: Ch 1, sc in same sc and in each rem sc. Do not join.

Rnds 16–21: Rep Rnd 15.

Rnd 22: Ch 1, sc in same sc and in each rem sc, join in first sc.
Fasten off. ❧

Mesh Stitch

Just chains and single crochets are combined to fashion this lovely lacy-look stitch pattern

Knit

Crochet

Crochet Stitch Pattern

Multiple of 5 sts + 1

Row 1: Ch 6, sc in 2nd ch from hook and in each ch across, turn. *(5 sc)*

Row 2: Ch 4 (counts as a dc and a ch-1 sp), sk next sc, dc in next sc, ch 1, sk next sc, dc in next sc, turn.

Row 3: Ch 1, sc in each dc and in each ch, turn.

Rep Rows 2 and 3 for pattern.

Mesh Stitch Scarf

Design by Darla Sims

The open-mesh rows become lacy stripes when combined with pretty multicolored rows of short eyelash yarn. This scarf is light and fun to wear even when you don't need an overcoat.

 INTERMEDIATE

Finished Size
Approximately 3 x 64 inches

Materials
Patons Cha Cha bulky (chunky) weight yarn:
    1¾ oz/77 yds/50g
      #02002 vegas (A)

5 BULKY

Patons Katrina medium (worsted) weight yarn:
    3½ oz/163 yds/100g
      #10128 dawn (B)
Size J/10/6mm or size needed to obtain gauge

4 MEDIUM

Gauge
11 sts = 3 inches

Scarf
Row 1: With A, loosely ch 12; sc in 2nd ch from hook and in each rem ch, turn. (11 sc)

Row 2: Ch 1, sc in each sc, turn.

Rows 3–10: Rep Row 2. At end of Row 10, change to B.

Rows 11–13: Rep Row 2.

Row 14: Ch 4 (counts as a dc and a ch-1 sp), sk next sc, dc in next sc, *ch 1, sk next sc, dc in next sc; rep from * 3 times more, turn.

Row 15: Ch 1, sc in each dc and in each ch, turn.

Rows 16 & 17: Rep Row 2.

Row 18: Ch 4, sk next sc, dc in next sc, *ch 1, sk next sc, dc in next sc; rep from * 3 times more, turn.

Rows 19–21: Rep Rows 15–17. At end of Row 21, change to A.

Rows 22–41: Rep Row 2. At end of Row 41, change to B.

Rows 42–52: Rep Rows 11–21. At end of Row 52, change to A.

Rows 53–56: Rep Row 2. At end of Row 56, change to B.

Rows 57–67: Rep Rows 11–21. At end of Row 67, change to A.

Rows 68–75: Rep Row 2. At end of Row 75, change to B.

Rows 76–86: Rep Rows 11–21. At end of Row 84, change to A.

Rows 87–92: Rep Row 2. At end of Row 90, change to B.

Rows 93–103: Rep Rows 11–21. At end of Row 99, change to A.

Rows 104–113: Rep Row 2. At end of Row 109, change to B.

Rows 114–124: Rep Rows 11–21. At end of Row 118, change to A.

Continued on page 162

Drop Stitch

Your finger becomes the tool for creating this enthralling drop-stitch pattern.

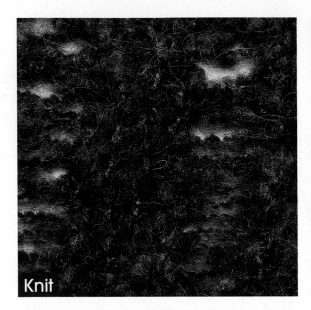

Knit

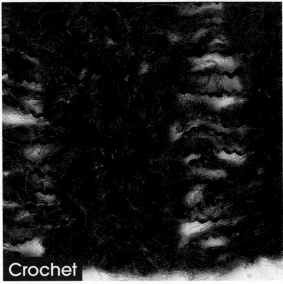

Crochet

Crochet Stitch Pattern

Special Stitch

  For long loop (long lp), wrap yarn around pinkie finger of right hand.

Multiple of 2 sts + 1

Row 1: Loosely ch 3, sc in 2nd ch from hook and in each rem ch, turn. *(2 sc)*

Rows 2 & 3: Ch 1, sc in each sc, turn.

Row 4: Ch 1, **long lp** *(see Special Stitch)*, pull to right, sc in first sc; * long lp, sc in next sc, turn.

Row 5: Pull up lp even with hook, insert hook in first long lp, yo and draw lp through, yo and draw through both long
lp and hook on hook; *insert hook in next long lp, yo and draw lp through, yo and draw through both long lp and hook on hook, turn.

Rep Rows 2–5 for pattern.

Drop-Stitch Scarf

Design by Darla Sims

Star quality shines through in this glamorous scarf made with open drop-stitch pattern in a luscious mohair-blend yarn.

 **INTERMEDIATE**

Finished Size
Approximately 7 x 64 inches, excluding fringe.

Materials
Patons Divine bulky (chunky) weight yarn:
    3½ oz/142 yds/100g
      #06430 richest rose
Size M/13/9mm or size needed to obtain gauge

Gauge
3 sc = 2 inches

Scarf
Row 1: Loosely ch 11, sc in 2nd ch from hook and in each rem ch, turn. *(10 sc)*

Rows 2 & 3: Ch 1, sc in each sc, turn.

Row 4: Ch 1, **long lp** *(see Special Stitch on page 160)*, pull to right, sc in first sc; *long lp, sc in next sc; rep from * across, turn.

Row 5: Pull up lp even with hook, insert hook in first long lp, yo and draw lp through, yo and draw through both long lp and hook on hook; *insert hook in next long lp, yo and draw lp through, yo and draw through both long lp and hook on hook; rep from * 8 times more, turn.

Rep Rows 2–5 until scarf measures approximately 64 inches in length, ending with a Row 3. Fasten off.

Fringe
For fringe, cut twenty 12-inch strands. Pull one strand through each st across each short end and knot for fringe. ❖

Mesh Stitch Scarf
Continued from 158

Rows 125–128: Rep Row 2. At end of Row 127, change to B.

Rows 129–139: Rep Rows 11–21. At end of Row 131, change to A.

Rows 140–155: Rep Rows 2. At end of Row 140, change to B.

Rows 156–166: Rep Rows 11–21. At end of Row 156, change to A.

Rows 167–176: Rep Row 2. Fasten off. ❖

Alternating Stitch

Long single crochet stitches worked into previous rows create
a look that mimics knitted alternating slip stitches.

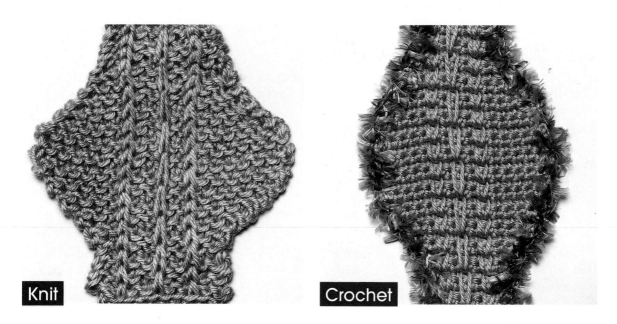

Knit

Crochet

Crochet Stitch Pattern

Special Stitch

For **long single crochet (long sc)**, pull up lp in st and row indicated to height of working row, complete as sc.

Row 1: Loosely ch 8, sc in 2nd ch from hook and in each rem ch, turn. *(7 sc)*

Row 2 & all even-numbered rows: Ch 1, sc in each sc, turn.

Row 3: Ch 1, sc in first sc, **long sc** *(see Special Stitch)* in sc below next sc, sc in next 3 sc, long sc in sc below next sc, sc in next sc, turn.

Row 5: Ch 1, sc in first sc, long sc in next long sc on row below, sc in next sc, long sc in next sc 3 rows below next sc, sc in next sc, long sc in next long sc on row below, sc in next sc, turn.

Rep Rows 2–5 for pattern.

Alternating & Undulating Scarf

Design by Darla Sims

Fun and funky describes this wonderful scarf! The Alternating and Undulating stitch patterns are combined to give it spunk, with novelty edging and fringe added for extra style.

 **EASY**

Finished Size
Approximately 5 x 60 inches, including fringe

Materials
Spinrite Bernat Satin medium (worsted) weight yarn:
3½ oz/163 yds/100g
#04423 flamingo (A)
Spinrite Bernat Boa bulky (chunky) weight yarn:
1¾ oz/71 yds/50g
#081420 love bird (B)
Size H/8/5mm or size needed to obtain gauge

Gauge
7 sts = 2 inches

Scarf
Row 1 (RS): With A, loosely ch 8, sc in 2nd ch from hook and in each rem ch, turn. *(7 sc)*

Row 2 & all even-numbered rows: Ch 1, sc in each sc, turn.

Row 3: Ch 1, sc in first sc, **long sc** *(see Special Stitch on page 163)* in sc below next sc, sc in next 3 sc, long sc in sc below next sc, sc in next sc, turn.

Row 5: Ch 1, sc in first sc, long sc in next long sc on row below, sc in next sc, long sc in next sc 3 rows below next sc, sc in next sc, long sc in next long sc on row below, sc in next sc, turn.

Row 7: Ch 1, sc in first sc, long sc in next long sc, sc in next 3 sc, long sc in next long sc, sc in next sc, turn.

Row 9: Ch 1, 2 sc in first sc, long sc in next long sc, sc in next sc, long sc in next sc 3 rows below next sc, sc in next sc, long sc in next long sc, 2 sc in next sc, turn.

Row 11: Ch 1, 2 sc in first sc, sc in next sc, long sc in next long sc, sc in next 3 sc, long sc in next long sc, sc in next sc, 2 sc in next sc, turn.

Row 13: Ch 1, 2 sc in first sc, long sc in sc below next sc, sc in next sc, long sc in next long sc, sc in next sc, long sc in next sc 3 rows below next sc, sc in next sc, long sc in next long sc, sc in next sc, long sc in next long sc, 2 sc in next sc, turn.

Row 15: Ch 1, 2 sc in first sc, [sc in next sc, long sc in next long sc] 2 times, sc in next 3 sc, [long sc in next long sc, sc in next sc] 2 times, 2 sc in next sc, turn.

Row 17: Ch 1, 2 sc in first sc, long sc in sc below next sc, sc in next sc, [long sc in next long sc, sc in next sc] 2 times, long sc in next sc 3 rows below next sc, [sc in next sc, long sc in next long sc] 2 times, sc in next sc, long sc in next long sc, 2 sc in next sc, turn.

Row 19: Ch 1, 2 sc in first sc, [sc in next sc, long sc in next long sc] 3 times, sc in next 3 sc, [long sc in next long sc, sc in next sc] 3 times, 2 sc in next sc, turn.

Row 21: Ch 1, 2 sc in first sc, long sc in sc below next sc, sc in next sc, [long sc in next long sc, sc in next sc] 3 times, long sc in next sc 3 rows below next sc, [sc in next sc, long sc in next long sc] 3 times, sc in next sc, long sc in next long sc, 2 sc in next sc, turn.

Row 23: Ch 1, sc in first 2 sc, [long sc in next long sc, sc in next sc] 4 times, sc in next 2 sc, [long sc in next long sc, sc in next sc] 4 times, sc in next sc, turn.

Row 25: Ch 1, sc in first 2 sc, [long sc in next long sc, sc in next sc] 4 times, long sc in next sc 3 rows below next sc, [sc in next sc, long sc in next long sc] 4 times, sc in next sc, turn.

Row 27: Rep Row 23.

Row 29: Rep Row 25.
*Note: For **sc dec**, pull up lp in 2 sts indicated, yo and draw through all 3 lps on hook.*

Row 31: Ch 1, **sc dec** *(see Note)* over first 2 sc, [long sc in next long sc, sc in next sc] 4 times, sc in next 2 sc, [long sc in next long sc, sc in next sc] 3 times, long sc in next long sc, sc dec over last 2 sc, turn.

Row 33: Ch 1, sc dec, sc in next sc, [long sc in next long sc, sc in next sc] 3 times, long sc in next sc 3 rows below next sc, [sc in next sc, long sc in next long sc] 3 times; sc in next sc, sc dec, turn.

Row 35: Ch 1, sc dec, [long sc in next long sc, sc in next sc] 3 times, sc in next 2 sc, [long sc in next long sc, sc in next sc] 2 times, long sc in next long sc, sc dec, turn.

Row 37: Ch 1, sc dec, sc in next sc, [long sc in next long sc, sc in next sc] 2 times, long sc in next sc 3 rows below next sc, [sc in next sc, long sc in next long sc] 2 times, sc in next sc, sc dec, turn.

Row 39: Ch 1, sc dec; long sc in next long sc, sc in next sc, long sc in next long sc, sc in next 3 sc, long sc in next long sc, sc in next sc, long sc in next long sc, sc dec, turn.

Row 41: Ch 1, sc dec, sc in next sc, long sc in next long sc, sc in next sc, long sc in next sc 3 rows below next sc, sc in next sc, long sc in next long sc, sc in next sc, sc dec, turn.

Row 43: Ch 1, sc dec, long sc in next long sc, sc in next 3 sc, long sc in next long sc, sc in next sc, turn.

Row 44: Ch 1, sc in each sc, turn.

[Rep Rows 5–44] 5 times more.

Rep Rows 3–8.
Fasten off.

Edging
Hold piece with RS facing you and beg ch at top; join B in first unused lp of beg ch; ch 1, sc in same lp, working in rem unused lps of beg ch, sc in each lp, in ends of rows along next side, in sc of last row and in ends of rows on next side; join in first sc.
Fasten off.

Fringe
For **fringe**, cut 28 (12-inch) strands of B. Pull 2 strands through each st across each short end and knot for fringe. ❖

Band of Feathers

Created in rows of single crochets and long single crochets,
this stitch forms vertical rows of featherlike stitches.

Knit

Crochet

Crochet Stitch Pattern

Special Stitch

  For long single crochet (long sc), pull up lp in st indicated on row below to height of working row, yo, draw through 2 lps on hook.

Multiple of 11 sts + 1

Row 1: Ch 12, sc in 2nd ch from hook and in each ch across, turn. *(11 sc)*

Rows 2–4: Ch 1, sc in each sc, turn.

Row 5: Ch 1, sc in first 2 sc, sk next 3 sc, **long sc** *(see Special Stitch)* in sc 3 rows below next sc, sc in next 5 sc, long sc in same sp as previous long sc made, sc in next 2 sc.

Row 6: Ch 1, sc in each sc, turn.

Rep Rows 2–6 for pattern.

Band-of-Feathers Handbag

Design by Darla Sims

Perfectly styled to take you from everyday activities to dinner in town, this purse works up quickly with two strands of worsted weight yarn.

 INTERMEDIATE

Finished Size
Approximately 7 x 10 inches, excluding handles

Materials
Lion Brand Wool-Ease medium (worsted) weight yarn:
    6 oz/394 yds/170g #125 camel
Size J/10/6mm or size needed to obtain gauge
Yarn needle
Pair of plastic purse handles

Gauge
7 sts = 2 inches

Side (make 2)
Note: Hold 2 strands tog throughout.

Row 1 (RS): Loosely ch 30, sc in 2nd ch from hook and in each ch across, turn. *(29 sc)*

Rows 2–4: Ch 1, sc in each sc, turn.

Row 5: Ch 1, sc in first 2 sc, sk next 3 sc, **long sc** *(see Special Stitch on page 167)* in sc 3 rows below next sc, sc in next 5 sc, long sc in same sp as previous long sc made, sc in next 2 sc, *sk next 3 sc, long sc in sc 3 rows below next sc, sc in next 5 sc, long sc in same sp as previous long sc made, sc in next 2 sc; rep from * once more, turn.

Row 6: Ch 1, sc in each sc, turn.

[Rep Rows 2–6] 9 times.
Fasten off.

Flap
Row 1: Sk first 5 sc, join yarn with sl st in next sc, ch 1, sc in same sc and each sc to last 5 sc, turn, leaving rem sc unworked. *(19 sc)*

Row 2: Ch 1, sc in each sc, turn.
Rep Row 2 until flap fits around handle.
Fasten off.

Finishing
Hold pieces with WS tog; sew sides and bottom of handbag. Whipstitch flaps over handles. ♣

Cable in a Diamond

A small cable is cleverly added inside the diamond shape using front post double crochet stitches.

Knit

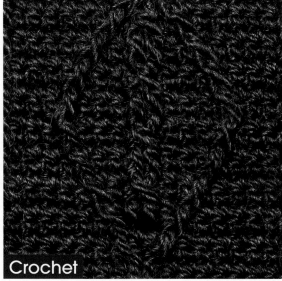

Crochet

Crochet Stitch Pattern

Special Stitch

    For front post double crochet (fpdc), yo, insert hook from front to back around **post** (*see Stitch Guide*) of st indicated, yo, draw lp through, [yo, draw through 2 lps on hook] 2 times. ***Note:*** *Sk st behind fpdc on working row.*

Multiple of 16 sts + 1

Row 1: With larger hook, loosely ch 17, sc in 2nd ch from hook and in each rem ch, turn. (*16 sc*)

Row 2 & all even-numbered rows: Ch 1, sc in each sc, turn.

Row 3: Rep Row 2.

Row 5: Ch 1, sc in next 7 sc, sk next sc, **fpdc** (*see Special Stitch*) around sc below next sc, fpdc around sc below skipped sc, sc in next 7 sc, turn.

Row 7: Ch 1, sc in next 6 sc, fpdc around next fpdc, sc in next 2 sc, fpdc around next fpdc, sc in next 6 sc, turn.

Row 9: Ch 1, sc in next 5 sc, fpdc around next fpdc, sc in next sc, fpdc around each of next 2 sc, sc in next sc, fpdc around next fpdc, sc in next 5 sc, turn.

Row 11: Ch 1, sc in next 4 sc, fpdc around next fpdc, sc in next 2 sc, sk next fpdc, fpdc around next fpdc, fpdc around skipped fpdc, sc in next 2 sc, fpdc around next fpdc, sc in next 4 sc, turn.

Row 13: Ch 1, sc in next 3 sc, fpdc around next fpdc, sc in next 3 sc, fpdc around each of next 2 fpdc, sc in next 3 sc, fpdc around next fpdc, sc in next 3 sc, turn.

Row 15: Ch 1, sc in next 2 sc, fpdc around next fpdc, sc in next 4 sc, sk next fpdc, fpdc around next fpdc, fpdc around skipped fpdc, sc in next 4 sc, fpdc around next fpdc, sc in next 3 sc, turn.

Row 17: Ch 1, sc in next 3 sc, fpdc around next fpdc, sc in next 3 sc, fpdc around each of next 2 fpdc, sc in next 3 sc, fpdc around next fpdc, sc in next 3 sc, turn.

Row 19: Ch 1, sc in next 4 sc, fpdc around next fpdc, sc in next 2 sc, sk next fpdc, fpdc around next st, fpdc around skipped fpdc, sc in next 2 sc, fpdc around next fpdc, sc in next 4 sc, turn.

Row 21: Ch 1, sc in next 5 sc, fpdc around next fpdc, sc in next sc, fpdc around each of next 2 sts, fpdc around next fpdc, sc in next sc, fpdc around next fpdc, sc in next 5 sc, turn.

Row 23: Ch 1, sc in next 6 sc, fpdc around next fpdc, sc in next 2 sc, sk next 2 fpdc, fpdc around next fpdc, sc in next 6 sc, turn.

Row 25: Ch 1, sc in next 7 sc, sk next fpdc, fpdc around next fpdc, fpdc around skipped fpdc, sc in next 7 sc, turn.

Row 27: Ch 1, sc in each st, turn.

Row 28: Ch 1, sc in each sc, turn.

Rep Rows 3–28 for pattern.

Cable-in-a-Diamond Purse

Design by Darla Sims

Great for gifts or for making at the last minute to accessorize a new outfit, this handy purse is high on style.

 **INTERMEDIATE**

Finished Size
Approximately 7 x 8 inches, excluding handles

Materials
Brown Sheep Lamb's Pride medium (worsted) weight yarn:

4 MEDIUM

    4 oz/190 yds/113g
      #M77 blue magic
Sizes H/8/5mm and G/6/4mm or sizes needed to obtain gauge
Yarn needle
Pair of wooden purse handles

Gauge
7 sts = 2 inches

Side (make 2)
Row 1: With larger hook, loosely ch 27, sc in 2nd ch from hook and in each rem ch, turn. *(26 sc)*

Row 2 & all even-numbered rows: Ch 1, sc in each sc, turn.

Row 3: Ch 1, sc in next 4 sc, **fpdc** *(see Special Stitch on page 170)* around sc below next sc, sc in next 16 sc, fpdc around sc below next sc, sc in next 4 sc, turn.

Row 5: Ch 1, sc in next 4 sc, fpdc around next fpdc, sc in next 7 sc, sk next sc, fpdc around sc below next sc, fpdc around sc below skipped sc, sc in next 7 sc, fpdc around sc below next sc, sc in next 4 sc, turn.

Row 7: Ch 1, sc in next 4 sc, fpdc around next fpdc, sc in next 6 sc, fpdc around next fpdc, sc in next 2 sc, fpdc around next fpdc, sc in next 6 sc, fpdc around next fpdc, sc in next 4 sc, turn.

Row 9: Ch 1, sc in next 4 sc, fpdc around next fpdc, sc in next 5 sc, fpdc around next fpdc, sc in next sc, fpdc around each of next 2 sc, sc in next sc, fpdc around next fpdc, sc in next 5 sc, fpdc around next fpdc, sc in next 4 sc, turn.

Row 11: Ch 1, sc in next 4 sc, fpdc around next fpdc, sc in next 4 sc, fpdc around next fpdc, sc in next 2 sc, sk next fpdc, fpdc around next fpdc, fpdc around skipped fpdc, sc in next 2 sc, fpdc around next fpdc, sc in next 4 sc, fpdc around next fpdc, sc in next 4 sc, turn.

Row 13: Ch 1, sc in next 4 sc, fpdc around next fpdc, sc in next 3 sc, fpdc around next fpdc, sc in next 3 sc, fpdc around each of next 2 fpdc, sc in next 3 sc, fpdc around next fpdc, sc in next 3 sc, fpdc around next fpdc, sc in next 4 sc, turn.

Row 15: Ch 1, sc in next 4 sc, fpdc around next fpdc, sc in next 2 sc, fpdc around next fpdc, sc in next 4 sc, sk next fpdc, fpdc around next fpdc, fpdc around skipped fpdc, sc in next 4 sc, fpdc around next fpdc, sc in next 2 sc, fpdc around next fpdc, sc in next 4 sc, turn.

Row 17: Ch 1, sc in next 4 sc, fpdc around next fpdc, sc in next 3 sc, fpdc around next fpdc, sc in next 3 sc, fpdc around each of next 2 fpdc, sc in next 3 sc, fpdc around next fpdc, sc in next 3 sc, fpdc around next fpdc, sc in next 4 sc, turn.

Row 19: Ch 1, sc in next 4 sc, fpdc around next fpdc, sc in next 4 sc, fpdc around next fpdc, sc in next 2 sc, sk next fpdc, fpdc around next st, fpdc around skipped fpdc, sc in next 2 sc, fpdc around next fpdc, sc in next 4 sc, fpdc around next fpdc, sc in next 4 sc, turn.

Row 21: Ch 1, sc in next 4 sc, fpdc around next fpdc, sc in next 5 sc, fpdc around next fpdc, sc in next sc, fpdc around each of next 2 sts, fpdc around next fpdc, sc in next sc, fpdc around next fpdc, sc in next 5 sc, fpdc around next fpdc, sc in next 4 sc, turn.

Row 23: Ch 1, sc in next 4 sc, fpdc around next fpdc, sc in next 6 sc, fpdc around next fpdc, sc in next 2 sc, sk next 2 fpdc, fpdc around next fpdc, sc in next 6 sc, fpdc around next fpdc, sc in next 4 sc, turn.

Row 25: Ch 1, sc in next 4 sc, fpdc around next fpdc, sc in next 7 sc, sk next fpdc, fpdc around next fpdc, fpdc around skipped fpdc, sc in next 7 sc, fpdc around next fpdc, sc in next 4 sc, turn.

Row 27: Ch 1, sc in next 4 sc, fpdc around next fpdc, sc in next 16 sc, fpdc around next fpdc, sc in next 4 sc. Fasten off.

Edging

Rnd 1: With smaller hook, sc around edges of sides, working 3 sc in each corner, join with sl st in first sc.

Rnd 2: Ch 1, working left to right, reverse sc in each sc; join in first reverse sc. Fasten off.

Hold sides with WS tog. Sew sides tog below Rnd 2 of edging, leaving upper edge open. Sew handles to purse. ❧

Abbreviations & Symbols

beg ....begin/beginning
bpdc .... back post double crochet
bphdc............ back post half double crochet
bpsc...................... back post single crochet
bptr .... back post treble crochet
CC ....contrasting color
ch...chain stitch
ch-.................................... refers to chain or
.... space previously made (i.e. ch-1 space)
cl...cluster
cm......................................centimeter(s)
dc...double crochet
dec ....decrease/decreases/decreasing
dtr .... double treble crochet
fpdc...................... front post double crochet
fphdc............ front post half double crochet
fpsc .... front post single crochet
fptr .... front post treble crochet
g... gram(s)
hdc.............................. half double crochet
lp(s).. loop(s)
MC .... main color
mm ....millimeter(s)
oz ....ounce(s)
rem .... remain/remaining
rep...repeat(s)
rnd(s) ....round(s)
RS .... right side
sc...single crochet
sk ....skip
sl st..slip stitch
sp(s) .... space(s)

st(s) .... stitch(es)
tog... together
tr ....treble crochet
trtr .... triple treble crochet
WS.. wrong side
yd(s) .... yard(s)
yo.. yarn over

* An asterisk is used to mark the beginning of a portion of instructions to be worked more than once; thus, "rep from * twice more" means after working the instructions once, repeat the instructions following the asterisk twice more (3 times in all).

( ) Parentheses enclose instructions which are to be worked the number of times indicated after the parentheses. For example, "(2 dc in next st, sk next st) 5 times" means to follow the instructions within the parentheses a total of five times. Parentheses may also be used to enclose a group of stitches which should be worked in one space or stitch. For example, "(2dc, ch2, 2 dc) in next st" means to work all the stitches within the parentheses in the next stitch.

[ ] Brackets are used in the same manner as asterisks. Follow the specific instructions given when repeating.

Join—join with a slip stitch unless otherwise specified.

Standard Yarn Weight System

Categories of yarn, gauge ranges, and recommended needle and hook sizes

Yarn Weight Symbol & Category Names	1 SUPER FINE	2 FINE	3 LIGHT	4 MEDIUM	5 BULKY	6 SUPER BULKY
Type of Yarns in Category	Sock, Fingering, Baby	Sport, Baby	DK, Light Worsted	Worsted, Afghan, Aran	Chunky, Craft, Rug	Bulky, Roving
Crochet Gauge* Ranges in Single Crochet to 4 inch	21–32 sts	16–20 sts	12–17 sts	11–14 sts	8–11 sts	5–9 sts
Recommended Hook in Metric Size Range	2.25–3.5 mm	3.5–4.5 mm	4.5–5.5 mm	5.5–6.5 mm	6.5–9 mm	9 mm and larger
Recommended Hook U.S. Size Range	B1–E4	E4–7	7–I-9	I-9–K-10½	K-10½–M-13	M-13 and larger

* GUIDELINES ONLY: The above reflect the most commonly used gauges and hook sizes for specific yarn categories.

Skill Levels

BEGINNER
Beginner projects for first-time crocheters using basic stitches. Minimal shaping.

EASY
Easy projects using basic stitches, repetitive stitch patterns, simple color changes and simple shaping and finishing.

INTERMEDIATE
Intermediate projects with a variety of stitches, mid-level shaping and finishing.

EXPERIENCED
Experienced projects using advanced techniques and stitches, detailed shaping and refined finishing.

Crochet Stitch Guide

STANDARD ABBREVIATIONS

beg . . . . beginning
ch, chs . . . . . chain, chains
dc . . . . double crochet
dec . . . . decrease
hdc . . . half double crochet
inc . . . . increase
lp, lps . . . . loop, loops
rnd, rnds . . round, rounds
sc . . . . single crochet
sl st . . . . slip stitch
sp, sps . . . . . space, spaces
st, sts . . . . . stitch, stitches
tog . . . . together
tr . . . . treble crochet
yo . . . . yarn over

sc next 2 sts tog......(insert hook in next st, yo, pull through st) 2 times, yo, pull through all 3 lps on hook.

hdc next 2 sts tog.....(yo, insert hook in next st, yo, pull through st) 2 times, yo, pull through all 5 lps on hook.

dc next 2 sts tog......(yo, insert hook in next st, yo, pull through 2 lps on hook) 2 times, yo, pull through all 3 lps on hook.

Chain—ch: Yo, pull through lp on hook.

Slip stitch—sl st: Insert hook in st, yo, pull through both lps on hook.

Single crochet—sc: Insert hook in st, yo, pull through st, yo, pull through both lps on hook.

Reverse single crochet—reverse sc: Working from left to right, insert hook in next st, complete as sc.

Front post stitch—fp: Back post stitch—bp: When working post st, insert hook from right to left around post of st on previous row.

Back   **Front**

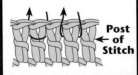

Post ← of Stitch

Front loop—front lp: Back loop—back lp:

Front Loop   **Back Loop**

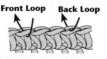

Half double crochet—hdc: Yo, insert hook in st, yo, pull through st, yo, pull through all 3 lps on hook.

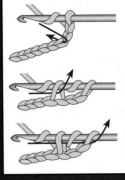

Double crochet—dc: Yo, insert hook in st, yo, pull through st, (yo, pull through 2 lps) 2 times.

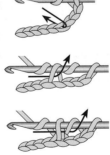

Treble crochet—tr: Yo 2 times, insert hook in st, yo, pull through st, (yo, pull through 2 lps) 3 times.

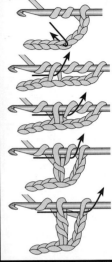

Double treble crochet—dtr: Yo 3 times, insert hook in st, yo, pull through st, (yo, pull through 2 lps) 4 times.

Change colors: Drop first color; with second color, pull through last 2 lps of st.

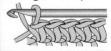

The patterns in this book are written using American crochet stitch terminology.
For our international customers, hook sizes, stitches and yarn definitions should be converted as follows:

But, as with all patterns,
test your gauge (tension) to be sure.

US	= INTERNATIONAL
sl st (slip stitch)	= sc (single crochet)
sc (single crochet)	= dc (double crochet)
hdc (half double crochet)	= htr (half treble crochet)
dc (double crochet)	= tr (treble crochet)
tr (treble crochet)	= dtr (double treble crochet)
dtr (double treble crochet)	= ttr (triple treble crochet)
skip	= miss

THREAD/YARNS

Bedspread Weight	= No. 10 Cotton or Virtuoso
Sport Weight	= 4 Ply or thin DK
Worsted Weight	= Thick DK or Aran

MEASUREMENTS

1" = 2.54 cm
1 yd. = .9144 m
1 oz. = 28.35 g

CROCHET HOOKS

Metric	US	Metric	US
.60mm	14	3.00mm	D/3
.75mm	12	3.50mm	E/4
1.00mm	10	4.00mm	F/5
1.50mm	6	4.50mm	G/6
1.75mm	5	5.00mm	H/8
2.00mm	B/1	5.50mm	I/9
2.50mm	C/2	6.00mm	J/10

From
Knit to
Crochet